The Essential Air Fryer Cookbook uk

Delicious and Healthy Recipes for Quick and Easy Air Frying in the UK

Logan Gentry

Introduction

Welcome to the exciting world of air frying with our *Air Fryer Cookbook UK* edition. This cookbook is your go-to guide for exploring the endless possibilities of air frying and creating delicious, crispy, and healthier meals right in your own kitchen. Whether you're new to air frying or a seasoned pro, this cookbook will inspire you to make the most of this versatile kitchen appliance.

Air frying has taken the culinary world by storm, offering a healthier alternative to traditional deep-frying methods. With the power of hot air circulation, you can achieve that desirable crispy texture and golden-brown finish, all while using significantly less oil. It's a game-changer for those who want to enjoy their favorite fried foods guilt-free.

In this cookbook, we've curated a wide range of recipes specifically tailored to the UK audience, considering the regional flavors, ingredients, and culinary preferences. From classic British dishes with a healthier twist to international cuisines that will take your taste buds on a global adventure, you'll find a variety of recipes that will suit every palate.

We believe that cooking should be enjoyable, and that's why our recipes are designed to be accessible and easy to follow. You don't need to be a professional chef to create incredible meals with your air fryer. Whether you're cooking for yourself, your family, or entertaining guests, our recipes will guide you through each step, ensuring your success in the kitchen.

In addition to delicious recipes, this cookbook provides useful tips and tricks for getting the most out of your air fryer. You'll learn about optimal cooking times and temperatures, how to properly preheat your air fryer, and tips for achieving that perfect crispy texture. We've also included suggestions for ingredient substitutions and ways to make your favorite recipes even healthier.

Embracing air frying means embracing a healthier lifestyle, and we're here to support you on your journey. From appetizers and snacks to main courses and desserts, you'll discover a wide array of recipes that will transform the way you cook and eat. Get ready to create meals that are not only delicious but also nutritious, without compromising on taste or texture.

So, let's dive into the world of air frying together. With our *Air Fryer Cookbook UK* edition, you'll unlock the full potential of your air fryer and elevate your culinary skills to new heights. Prepare to amaze yourself and your loved ones with mouthwatering, crispy creations that will make you fall in love with cooking all over again. Happy air frying!

Chapter 1 - How to Use an Air Fryer

An air fryer generally comes with the following components:

- Fry basket
- Outer basket
- Basket release button
- Sliding button guard
- Food divider
- Digital control panel
- Main housing unit

The air fryer's sliding button guard will prevent inadvertent presses of the release basket button. Without this feature, if the fry basket wasn't on a heat-resistant surface, the outer basket would detach from it and cause harm. Therefore, you shouldn't move the sliding button guard forward until both the outside basket and the frying basket are on a heat-resistant surface.

How to use the Control Panel

The On/Off Switch

The power button will turn on once the fry basket and the outer basket have been attached to the main housing unit. Typically, hitting the power button just once will set the device to its default temperature of 370 0F. By default, the cooking time will be 15 minutes. Cooking will start when the power button is pressed twice. The cooking will stop and the appliance will be turned off if the power button is hit once more while the process is in progress. After another 20 seconds, the blue fan icon will stop spinning, and the heat light will go out.

Timer Management

The cooking time can be changed by using the plus and minus signs. The time will change more quickly if you press and hold the button rather than one minute at a time.

Temperature regulation

The + and - signs allow you to adjust the temperature by 10°F increments. The temperature varies quickly as you click the button. 180 0F to 400 0F is the control range.

Default Button

Depending on the brand you choose, these features provide you the ability to select options. The cooking temperature and time are fixed and the cooking process begins when the desired preset is chosen. Manually adjusting the temperature and time will also overrule these preset parameters. Steak, fish, shrimp, and chicken would all be presets, as well as roast, fries, and baking.

Displays indicating the time and temperature make it easier to maintain track of the temperature and remaining cooking time. The blue fan icon begins spinning when the device is turned on, then after 20 seconds it stops. The preheat and cook mode is indicated by the red heat indicator.

Try out several recipes when you first start using an air fryer. The preset function is not required. If you want to cook quickly, you might try preheating the fryer. Choose a cooking period of 3 to 4 minutes, and aim for the default temperature. The frying basket and the outer basket must then be placed inside the main unit.

General Guidelines

Remove all packaging, labels, and stickers before using any air fryer for the first time. Use warm, soapy water to wash the fry and outer baskets. Most of the baskets are dishwasher safe. Use a clean, moist towel to wipe the cooking area's exterior and interior. Never wash the fryer or submerge it in water. Never overfill the outer basket with oil because the fryer only uses hot air to cook food.

Table of Contents

Introduction 3

Chapter 1 - How to Use an Air Fryer 4

Chapter 2 - Air Fryer Breakfast Recipes 11

Tex-Mex Hash Browns 11

Cajun Breakfast Sausage 12

Air Fryer Ham, Cheese, and Egg Salad Sandwich 13

French Toast Sticks with Berries 14

Air Fryer Vegan French "Toast" 15

Air Fryer Breakfast Biscuit Bombs 16

Chapter 3 - Air Fryer Appetizers/Snacks 18

Baked Spicy Chicken Meatballs 18

French Fries 19

Air Fryer Mozzarella Balls 20

Vegan Buffalo Cauliflower 21

Sweet Potato Tots 22

Potato Hay 23

Avocado Fries 24

Asian-Inspired Deviled Eggs 25

Loaded Greek Feta Fries 26

Crunchy Air-Fried Corn Dog Bites 28

Sweet Potato Fries 29

Chapter 4 - Chicken Recipes 30

Tandoori Chicken 30

Baked Thai Peanut Chicken Egg Rolls 31

Air Fryer Chicken Nuggets 32

Chick-fil-A Chicken Sandwich 33

Chicken Fried Rice 35

Southwest Chicken Salad 35

Chicken Shawarma Bowl 37

General Tso Chicken 38

Potato Chip Chicken 40

Calzones 41

Chicken Wings 42

Spicy Chicken Thighs 43

Ranch Chicken Tenders 44

Chapter 5 - Beef Recipes **45**

Roast Beef 45

Beef Empanadas 46

Easy Spring Rolls 48

Meat Loaf 49

Mock Taco Bell Crunch Wraps 50

Air Fryer Steak 51

Air-Fried Taco Dogs 52

Air Fryer Steak Tips 53

Cheeseburgers 54

Steak and Mushrooms 55

Chapter 6 - Pork Recipes **56**

Easy Air Fryer Pork Chops 56

Breaded Pork Chops 57

Pork Dumplings with Dipping Sauce 58

Herb-Crusted Pork Chops 60

Air-Fried Bacon 60

Korean Grilled Pork Dae Ji Bulgogi 61

Raspberry Balsamic Smoked Pork Chops 62

Pork Chops and Broccoli 63

Pork Chops with Brussels Sprouts 64

Chapter 7 - Lamb Recipes **65**

Greek Lamb and Spinach Meatballs with Tzatziki 65

Lamb Chops with Garlic Sauce 67

Lamb Roast with Potatoes, Carrots, and Sweet Potatoes 68

Classic Rack of Lamb (Herbs) 69

Roast Lamb Rack with Lemon and Cumin Crust 70

Spicy Lamb Sirloin Steak 71

Braised Lamb Shanks 72

Brussels Sprouts and Potato Quenelles 73

Mojito Lamb Kabobs 74

Chapter 8 – Seafood Recipes 74

Air Fryer Salmon 75

Salmon Cakes 76

Healthy Baked Salmon 77

Fish Tacos 78

Shrimp Spring Rolls with Sweet Chili Sauce 79

Air Fryer Lemon Pepper Shrimp 81

Shrimp Fried Rice 82

Air Fryer Scallops 83

Southern Style Catfish with Green Beans 84

Roasted Salmon with Fennel Salad 85

Fish en Papillote 86

Fish and Chips 87

Chapter 9 - Seafood Recipes 89

Coconut Shrimp 89

Hot and Sweet Coconut Shrimp and Apricot Sauce 90

Crab Cakes 91

Shrimp Scampi 93

Chapter 10 - Meatless and Vegan Recipes 94

French Fry Po' Boy (Cajun) 94

Sticky Mushroom Rice 95

Herb and Cheese Frittata 96

Grilled American Cheese Sandwich 97

Crispy Toasted Sesame Tofu 98

Twice-Fried Vegan Stuffed Potatoes 100

Easy Seitan Riblets 101

Crispy Vegetable Quesadilla 102

Vegetarian Tacos 103

Chapter 11 - Side Dish Recipes 104

Loaded Potatoes 104

Baked Garlic Parsley Potatoes 106

Cauliflower Stir-Fry 107

Crispy Onion Rings 108

Baked Sweet Potato 109

Herbed Brussels Sprouts 110

Cilantro Ranch Sweet Potato Cauliflower Patties 111

Garlic Bread 112

Potatoes Au Gratin 113

Roasted Broccoli with Cheese Sauce 114

Roasted Asian Broccoli 115

Chapter 12 - Pizzas and Pasta Recipes **116**

Whole-Wheat Pita Pizzas 116

Deep-Dish Pepperoni Pizza 117

Eggplant Parmesan Mini Pizzas 118

Margherita Pizza 120

Roasted Vegetable Pasta Salad 121

Mascarpone Mushroom Pasta 122

Air Fryer Ravioli 123

Green Curry Noodles 124

Chapter 13 - Desserts **126**

Nutella S'mores 126

Chocolate Cake 127

Cinnamon Apple Chips with Almond Yogurt Dip 128

Chocolate Chip Oatmeal Cookies 129

Banana Bread / Banana Muffins 130

Strawberry "Pop Tarts" 131

Churros with Chocolate Sauce 133

Doughnuts 134

Peach Pies 136

Double-Glazed Cinnamon Biscuit Bites 137

Chapter 14 – Air Fryer Breakfast Recipes **138**

Blueberry Muffins (Gluten-Free) 138

Breakfast Frittata 139

Breakfast Potatoes in the Air Fryer 140

Cheese and Veggie Egg Cups 141

Air-Fried Potato Hash 142

Toasted Sandwich 143

Chapter 15 - Air Fryer Appetizers/Snacks 144

Vegan Cheesy Potato Wedges 144

Mexican-Style Corn on the Cob 146

Spanakopita Bites 147

Falafels 148

Air Fryer Sweet Potato Chips 149

Potato Chips 150

Roasted Curry Chickpeas 151

Beet Chips 152

Kale Chips 153

Bow Tie Pasta Chips 154

Chapter 16 – Turkey Recipes 155

Air Fryer Turkey Bacon 155

Italian Meatballs 156

Herbed Turkey Breast 157

Turkey and Mushroom Patties 158

Olive-Brined Air-Fryer Turkey Breast 159

Greek Turkey Burgers 160

Turkey-Stuffed Peppers 161

Almond-Crusted Turkey Cutlets 162

Conclusion 164

Chapter 2 - Air Fryer Breakfast Recipes

Tex-Mex Hash Browns

Time needed for prep: 15 minutes

Time needed to cook: 30 minutes

Serves: 2

Nutritional values per serving:

Calories: 186

Fat: 4.3 g

Carb: 33.7 g

Fiber Content: 4.8 g

Total Protein: 4 g

Ingredients:

- ¾ pd potatoes, peeled, chop into one" cubes
- half red peppers, deseeded, chop into one" pieces
- 1 small jalapeño, deseeded, chop into one" rings
- quarter tsp taco seasoning mix
- Salt as per taste
- Pepper as per taste
- 1 tbsp olive oil, divided
- 2 onions, chop into one" pieces
- quarter tsp cumin powder

Directions:

1. Fill a container with the chopped potatoes. Pour some ice water on it. Give it a 20-minute soak. Remove the water.

2. Use a kitchen towel to pat the potatoes dry.

3. Fill a container with potatoes. The potatoes should be well-tossed in half a tablespoon of oil.

4. Insert the air fryer basket with the potatoes inside.

5. Air-fry the potatoes for 15 to 18 minutes, or until they are tender, in a preheated air fryer at 320 °F. Halfway through the frying process, shake the basket.

6. Place onion, bell pepper, and jalapenos in a bowl. Over the vegetables, drizzle the remaining oil. Well, toss.

7. Season generously with salt, pepper, cumin, and taco seasoning.

8. Stir in the potatoes thoroughly.

9. Pour the bowl's contents into the air fryer.

10. Increase the air fryer's temperature to 355 °F.

11. Cook the potatoes for 10 to 12 minutes, or until they are crisp and golden. While it is cooking, shake the basket a couple of times.

Cajun Breakfast Sausage

Time needed for prep: 5 minutes

Time needed to cook: 40 minutes

Serves: 6

Nutritional values per serving:

Calories: 126

Fat: 4.5 g

Carb: 11.5 g

Fiber Content: 1 g

Total Protein: 11 g

Ingredients:

- o ¾ pd ground sausage (chicken sausage or lean pork)
- o 1 tsp minced fresh thyme leaves or quarter-half tsp dried thyme
- o quarter tsp paprika
- o quarter tsp cayenne pepper
- o half tsp chopped sage (optional)
- o 1half tsps crushed garlic
- o Herbs of your choice, minced (optional)
- o half tsp chili flakes
- o half tsp onion powder
- o Salt as per taste
- o Pepper as per taste
- o 1 tsp brown sugar or maple syrup or coconut palm sugar

o 1 tsp Tabasco sauce, plus extra to taste

Directions:

1. Place ground sausage, all the herbs, and all the spices in a bowl of ice water.

2. With your hands, thoroughly combine. Add Tabasco sauce and stir.

3. Divide the mixture into 6 equal amounts and form each into a patty with a thickness of approximately 1-12 inches. Put them on a baking sheet that has been lined. Batch-air fry food.

4. Put two or three patties in the air fryer basket at once.

5. Air fried for 20 minutes at 370 °F in a preheated air fryer. Halfway through frying, flip the sides.

6. Top with hot sauce and Tabasco.

Air Fryer Ham, Cheese, and Egg Salad Sandwich

Time needed for prep: 5 minutes

Time needed to cook: 5 minutes

Serves: 2

Nutritional values per serving:

Calories: 722

Fat: 37 g

Carb: 59 g

Fiber Content: 3 g

Total Protein: 34 g

Ingredients:

o 2 bagels, sliced into 2 halves horizontally
o 2 slices Colby-Jack cheese
o 2 slices deli ham

For avocado-egg salad:

o 3 hard-boiled eggs, peeled, diced
o 1 tsp Dijon mustard
o Salt as per taste
o 2 tbsps mayonnaise
o 1 small avocado, peeled, pitted, diced

o   Paprika to taste

Directions:

1. To create the avocado salad, put the eggs, mayonnaise, mustard, salt, avocado, and paprika in a bowl. Stir to thoroughly blend. Put it to the side for a while.

2. In the meantime, top the bottom half of each bagel with a piece of ham and a slice of cheese. Put inside the basket of the air fryer. Place the bagels' top halves next to each other. If necessary, cook in batches.

3. Toast the bagels in an air fryer at 375 °F for 5 minutes, or to your preferred level of doneness.

4. Evenly distribute the avocado-egg salad and top with a cheese slice. Serve the sandwiches topped with the top halves of the bagels.

French Toast Sticks with Berries

Time needed for prep: 5 minutes

Time needed to cook: 7 minutes

Serves: 2

Nutritional values per serving:

Calories: 361

Fat: 10 g

Carb: 56 g

Fiber Content: 10 g

Total Protein: 14 g

Ingredients:

o   1 egg, beaten
o   half tsp vanilla extract
o   2 whole-grain bread slices, cut each into 4 long sticks
o   2 tbsps 2% reduced fat milk
o   quarter tsp cinnamon powder
o   ⅓ cup flaxseed meal
o   1 cup sliced fresh strawberries or blueberries
o   half tsp powdered sugar

- 2 tbsps packed light brown sugar, divided
- 4 tsps maple syrup, divided
- Cooking spray

Directions:

1. In a small bowl, whisk together the egg, cinnamon, 2 teaspoons maple syrup, vanilla, milk, and 1/2 tbsp brown sugar.

2. Fill another bowl with flaxseed meal and the leftover brown sugar.

3. Using the egg mixture, dip each of the strips. Shake to remove any extra egg. Apply the flaxseed mixture next. Apply frying spray to the coated breadsticks and arrange them in a single layer in the warm air fryer basket. If necessary, cook in batches.

4. Air fried for five minutes at 375 °F in a preheated air fryer.

5. Fry until golden brown on both sides, flipping once. Spray with cooking spray.

6. Place four breadsticks on each of the two platters. Overspread the sticks with strawberries. Add a teaspoon of maple syrup on top after that. Serve with a dusting of powdered sugar.

Air Fryer Vegan French "Toast"

Time needed for prep: 10 minutes

Time needed to cook: 30 minutes

Serves: 4

Nutritional values per serving:

Calories: 117

Fat: 13 g

Carb: 15 g

Fiber Content: 10 g

Total Protein: 25 g

Ingredients:

- 2 blocks tofu (extra firm), drained & excess moisture pressed out
- half cup granulated monk fruit sweetener
- 1 cup coconut flour

o   2 tbsps cinnamon powder

Directions:

1. Spread several layers of paper towels over the tofu for 10 to 15 minutes.

2. In a bowl, combine the coconut flour, cinnamon, and monk fruit sweetener. Stir well.

3. Horizontally slice each block of tofu into two equal pieces that are half an inch thick. Create two triangles out of each slice.

4. Place the tofu pieces in the air fryer basket after mixing them with the coconut flour mixture. Cook in groups.

5. Air fried for 14 minutes at 350 °F in a preheated air fryer.

6. Halfway through cooking, flip the sides.

7. Top with your preferred garnishes, such as berries, vegan cream, vegan sour cream, etc.

Air Fryer Breakfast Biscuit Bombs

Time needed for prep: 30 minutes

Time needed to cook: 18-20 minutes

Serves: 20

Nutritional values per serving:

Calories: 190

Fat: 13 g

Carb: 13 g

Fiber Content: 0 g

Total Protein: 7 g

Ingredients:

o   2 tbsps vegetable oil
o   4 eggs, beaten
o   Pepper as per taste
o   Salt as per taste
o   4 ounces sharp cheddar cheese, chop into 20 cubes of about half inch each
o   half pd bulk breakfast sausage

o   2 cans (10.2 ounces each) Flaky Layers biscuits that are refrigerated (10 biscuits in all)

For the egg wash:

- 2 tbsps water
- 2 eggs

Directions:

1. Cut two parchment paper sheets into two rounds each measuring about 8 inches in diameter.

2. Place a ring of parchment paper in the bottom of the air fryer basket.

3. Cooking spray should be used on the parchment paper.

4. When the heat is at medium-high, add a nonstick skillet. Oil is then heated. Sausage should not be pink after being added and cooked. As it cooks, break it simultaneously. With a spoon, remove and set aside in a container. Allow it to cool for a while.

5. Reduce the temperature to medium. Don't throw away the pan's fat.

6. Fill the skillet with the eggs. Taste and add salt and pepper as desired. Cook the eggs until they are soft-set, stirring often. Transfer to the sausage bowl. Mix thoroughly. Allow it to cool for a while.

7. Open the cans containing the dough. Cut each piece of dough into five biscuits. Separate each biscuit into two layers.

8. Form rounds from each layer that measure about 4 inches in diameter.

9. Fill each biscuit round with about a heaping tbsp of the meat mixture. Put a cheese cube on each.

10. Bring the edges together and cover the filling entirely. Firmly seal the edges by pressing them together. There will be a total of 20 biscuit bombs.

11. In a bowl, whisk eggs and water to form an egg wash. Egg wash should be applied evenly to the biscuits. batches when baking.

12. Place 5 biscuit bombs in the basket of the air fryer, seam side down.

13. Grease the other sheet of parchment paper on either side with cooking spray and place over the biscuit bombs. Place 5 biscuits over this sheet.

14. Air-fry in a pre-heated air fryer at 325 °F for 8 minutes.

15. Carefully remove the top parchment paper. Turn each biscuit and place the biscuits in a single layer. Cook for 4–8 minutes or until nice and golden brown.

16. Repeat steps 12–15 and cook the remaining biscuits.

Chapter 3 - Air Fryer Appetizers/Snacks

Baked Spicy Chicken Meatballs

Time needed for prep: 15 minutes

Time needed to cook: 10 minutes

Serves: 12 meatballs

Nutritional values per serving:

Calories: 47

Fat: 1 g

Carb: 4 g

Fiber Content: 0 g

Total Protein: 3 g

Ingredients:

- o For chicken meatballs:
- o half cup ground chicken
- o quarter cup chopped onion
- o Crushed chili flakes or chili powder to taste
- o Salt as per taste
- o quarter cup gluten-free oats flour
- o half tsp garlic powder or 2 cloves garlic, minced
- o half tbsp minced cilantro
- o For the teriyaki sauce:
- o 2 tbsps sweet-and-sour sauce
- o 1 tbsp light soy sauce
- o half tsp crushed chili flakes
- o half tsp ginger powder
- o half tsp garlic powder
- o 1 tbsp honey
- o 1 tbsp rice vinegar
- o Sesame seeds
- o Thinly sliced scallions

Directions:

1. To prepare chicken meatballs, combine all of the necessary ingredients in a bowl and thoroughly combine.

2. Divide it into 12 equal amounts and roll them into balls.

3. Put in the basket of the air fryer.

4. Bake for 8 to 10 minutes at 350 °F. Halfway through baking, shake the baking basket.

5. To prepare the sauce, place all of the necessary ingredients in a small pan. Once the heat is somewhat low, place the pan. Till the mixture becomes thick, stir continuously.

6. Add the meatballs and toss to thoroughly coat them.

7. Add sesame seeds and scallions as a garnish before serving.

French Fries

Time needed for prep: 30 minutes

Time needed to cook: 20-25 minutes

Serves: 2

Nutritional values per serving:

Calories: 189

Fat: 4.4 g

Carb: 34.3 g

Fiber Content: 2.5 g

Total Protein: 4.8 g

Ingredients:

- o 3 small russet potatoes, peeled, chop into fries
- o 1half tsps oil
- o 1 tbsp minced parsley
- o 1 tbsp parmesan cheese (grated)
- o Salt as per taste
- o Cooking spray

Directions:

1. Submerge the potatoes for 30 minutes in a container of cold water. The potatoes should be drained and dried with a kitchen towel.

2. Arrange the fries in a bowl and top with oil. Well, toss. Add salt, Parmesan, and parsley, then stir thoroughly.

3. Spray the air fryer basket with cooking spray liberally.

4. Insert into the basket of an air fryer. Distribute it evenly.

5. Air fried for 20 to 25 minutes at 360 °F in a preheated air fryer. While cooking, shake the basket a few times.

6. Present with your preferred dip.

Air Fryer Mozzarella Balls

Time needed for prep: 1 hour and 30 minutes

Time needed to cook: 10 minutes

Serves: 24

Nutritional values per serving: (1 ball):

Calories: 206

Fat: 14.6 g

Carb: 5.2 g

Fiber Content: 0.2 g

Total Protein: 13.3 g

Ingredients:

- o 4 cups freshly grated mozzarella
- o 2 eggs
- o 2 tbsps oregano
- o Salt as per taste
- o 6 tbsps cornflour
- o 2 cups Italian seasoned bread crumbs
- o 3 tsps garlic powder
- o 3 tbsps parmesan cheese (grated)

Directions:

1. Cover a baking sheet with a piece of parchment paper.

2. Combine cornflour, mozzarella, and Parmesan in a bowl by stirring well.

3. Divide the mixture into 24 equal sections and roll each portion into a ball. Place the baking sheet that has been prepared. For one hour, freeze.

4. In the meantime, mix the eggs thoroughly in a bowl.

5. Stir the bread crumbs, salt, and garlic powder in a separate basin.

6. Initially, dip each cheese ball individually in the egg mixture. Shake to remove any extra egg. Place the cheese balls on the baking sheet after dredging them in the mixture of bread crumbs.

7. Put in a 20-minute freeze. Cook in groups.

8. Pack the air fryer basket with as many items as will fit.

9. Air fried for 10 to 12 minutes at 400 °F in a preheated air fryer. While cooking, shake the basket a few times. The cheese balls should be removed from the air fryer once they start to melt. Allow the food to rest for two minutes before serving it after air frying.

10. Present with your preferred dip.

Vegan Buffalo Cauliflower

Time needed for prep: 10 minutes

Time needed to cook: 20 minutes

Serves: 2

Nutritional values per serving:

Calories: 201

Fat: 16 g

Carb: 11 g

Fiber Content: 1 g

Total Protein: 2 g

Ingredients:

For cauliflower:

- o   2 cups bite-sized cauliflower florets
- o   half tsp sea salt
- o   half cup bread crumbs (panko)

- o For buffalo coating:
- o 2 tbsps vegan buffalo sauce
- o 2 tbsps melted vegan butter
- o For dipping:
- o Vegan mayonnaise or any other dipping sauce of your choice

Directions:

1. To prepare Buffalo coating, combine buffalo sauce and melted vegan butter in a bowl and whisk.

2. To prepare breading, combine sea salt and panko in a basin and whisk.

3. Dip each cauliflower floret into the sauce mixture individually. Shake to remove extra mixture by shaking. Place in the air fryer basket after being dredged in the panko mixture.

4. Air fry without preheating the air fryer for 10 to 12 minutes at 400 °F. While cooking, shake the basket a few times.

5. Provide dipping sauce and serve hot.

Sweet Potato Tots

Time needed for prep: 20 minutes

Time needed to cook: 12-14 minutes

Serves: 2

Nutritional values per serving:

Calories: 78

Fat: 0 g

Carb: 19 g

Fiber Content: 2 g

Total Protein: 1 g

Ingredients:

- o 1 small sweet potato (7 ounces), peeled
- o Salt as per taste
- o half tbsp potato starch
- o A pinch garlic powder or to taste

- o 6 tbsps unsalted ketchup
- o Cooking spray

Directions:

1. Heat a small pot with water to a boil over medium heat.

Sweet potato should be added and cooked until fork-tender. Avoid overcooking.

3. Drain the water, then set the sweet potato aside to cool.

4. Sweet potatoes should be grated and set aside in a container. Garlic powder, salt, and potato starch should all be added.

5. Cut into tiny tots.

6. Spray cooking spray in the basket of the air fryer.

7. Arrange the tots in a single layer in the basket. The tots should be covered in oil.

8. Air-fry for 12 to 14 minutes at 400 °F in a preheated air fryer. Halfway through the frying process, shake the basket. Add some salt to it.

9. Immediately serve with ketchup.

Potato Hay

Time needed for prep: 10 minutes

Time needed to cook: 30 minutes

Serves: 2

Nutritional values per serving:

Calories: 113

Fat: 3.6 g

Carb: 18.6 g

Fiber Content: 2.3 g

Total Protein: 2.2 g

Ingredients:

- o   1 russet potato
- o   Salt as per taste
- o   Pepper as per taste
- o   half tbsp canola oil

Directions:

1. Use a spiralizer to create spirals out of the potato. Spirals should be cut into 3–4 inch lengths.

2. Place it in a container and fill it with water. Give it a 20-minute soak. Rinse after draining off the water.

3. Use paper towels to pat the potato spirals dry.

4. Oil the spirals with a thin layer. Season with salt and pepper. Well, toss.

5. Insert into the basket of an air fryer.

6. Air fried for five minutes at 360 °F in a preheated air fryer. Utilise tongs toss the potato hay.

7. Increase the heat to 390 °F. Fry until crisp and golden.

8. Present heat.

Avocado Fries

Time needed for prep: 15 minutes

Time needed to cook: 8 minutes

Serves: 2

Nutritional values per serving:

Calories: 262

Fat: 18 g

Carb: 23 g

Fiber Content: 7 g

Total Protein: 5 g

Ingredients:

- o   quarter cup flour (all purpose)
- o   1 egg, beaten

- o quarter cup bread crumbs (panko)
- o Salt as per taste
- o ¾ tsp pepper
- o half tbsp water
- o 1 avocado, peeled, pitted, chop into 8 slices
- o Cooking spray

For the dip:

- o 1 tbsp canola mayonnaise
- o half tbsp sriracha sauce
- o 2 tbsps unsalted ketchup
- o half tbsp apple cider vinegar

Directions:

1. In a bowl, combine the flour, salt, and pepper.

2. Put panko (bread crumbs) in a another bowl.

3. In a third bowl, thoroughly mix the egg and water.

4. Dip avocado slices into the flour mixture first. Then, cover it with egg mixture. Shake to remove any extra egg, then roll it in the bread crumbs. Fries should be placed in the air fryer basket.

5. Air-fry at 360 °F for 7-8 minutes, or until golden brown, in a preheated air fryer.

6. In the meantime, combine all of the dip's ingredients in a bowl by adding them there and stirring.

7. Distribute between 2 plates and offer dip.

Asian-Inspired Deviled Eggs

Time needed for prep: 15 minutes

Time needed to cook: 15 minutes

Serves: 6

Nutritional values per serving:

Calories: 63

Fat: 5.3 g

Carb: 0.8 g

Fiber Content: 0.1 g

Total Protein: 3.3 g

Ingredients:

- o   3 large eggs
- o   ¾ tsp sriracha sauce
- o   half tsp soy sauce (low-sodium)
- o   half tsp finely grated ginger
- o   Toasted sesame seeds to garnish
- o   1 tbsp mayonnaise
- o   ¾ tsp sesame oil
- o   half tsp Dijon mustard
- o   half tsp rice vinegar
- o   1 tbsp green onion (sliced fine)

Directions:

1. Put a trivet or air fryer rack inside the air fryer. Eggs should be put on the rack.

2. Air-fry for around 10-15 minutes at 260 °F.

3. Remove the eggs from the air fryer and place them in a bowl of ice water. Give it 10 minutes to sit in it.

4. After peeling, split each egg in half lengthwise.

5. Scoop the yolks out with a spoon and put them in a tiny blender jar. A few more ingredients to include are mayonnaise, sesame oil, sriracha sauce, Dijon mustard, soy sauce, ginger, and rice vinegar. until creamy, blend.

6. Put the mixture into a piping bag.

7. Insert the pipe into the tooth cavities.

8. Top with green onions and sesame seeds before serving.

Loaded Greek Feta Fries

Time needed for prep: 10 minutes

Time needed to cook: 30-40 minutes

Serves: 1

Nutritional values per serving:

Calories: 383

Fat: 16 g

Carb: 42 g

Fiber Content: 4 g

Total Protein: 19 g

Ingredients:

- o 1 Yukon gold potato or russet potato, scrubbed, pat dried, chop into fries
- o 1 tsp lemon zest (grated)
- o Salt as per taste
- o ⅛ tsp onion powder
- o ⅛ tsp garlic powder
- o quarter tsp oregano herbs (dry)
- o Pepper as per taste
- o ⅛ tsp paprika
- o 1 ounce skinless rotisserie chicken breast, shredded
- o 1 ounce feta cheese, finely grated
- o 2 tbsps prepared tzatziki
- o 1 tbsp chopped red onion
- o 1 small plum tomato, deseeded, diced
- o half tbsp chopped fresh oregano
- o half tbsp chopped fresh parsley
- o half tbsp olive oil
- o Cooking spray

Directions:

1. Spray cooking spray on the air fryer basket to grease it.

2. Add french fries to a bowl. Pour some oil on it. Well, toss.

3. Add salt, all the spices, dried oregano, and lemon zest. Toss to thoroughly coat.

4. Cook in groups.

5. Fry food in an air fryer that has been preheated to 380 °F for about 10-15 minutes, or until golden brown.

6. While the fries are frying, shake them a few times.

7. Before serving, reheat.

Fries should be put on a serving tray before assembly. Tzatziki, tomato, onion, feta, fresh herbs, and chicken should be distributed.

Crunchy Air-Fried Corn Dog Bites

Time needed for prep: 15 minutes

Time needed to cook: 10–12 minutes

Serves: 2

Nutritional values per serving: (3 corn dog bites with 2 tsps mustard):

Calories: 82

Fat: 3 g

Carb: 8 g

Fiber Content: 0 g

Total Protein: 5 g

Ingredients:

- o 1 uncured all-beef hot dog
- o quarter cup flour (all purpose)
- o ¾ cup finely crushed cornflakes cereal
- o 1 egg, lightly beaten
- o 4 tsps yellow mustard
- o Cooking spray

Directions:

1. Split the hot dog in half lengthwise first. Next, crosswise divide each half into three sections.

2. Insert one of the ends of each piece with six little bamboo skewers.

3. Whisk well after adding the egg to the bowl. In another bowl, add the flour. Fill a third bowl with cornflakes.

4. First, flour the pieces of hot dog. Dip next in the egg. Shake to remove any extra egg. Lastly, sprinkle with cornflakes. On adhere the cornflakes to the hot dog bits, lightly press.

5. Spray cooking spray on the air fryer basket to grease it.

6. Put the pieces of the corn dog in the air fryer basket. Use cooking spray to spritz.

7. Air-fry for 10 to 12 minutes, or until golden brown, at 375 °F in a preheated air fryer. At the midway point of frying, flip the hot dog bites.

Sweet Potato Fries

Time needed for prep: 10 minutes

Time needed to cook: 12-14 minutes

Serves: 2

Nutritional values per serving:

Calories: 104

Fat: 3 g

Carb: 17 g

Fiber Content: 3 g

Total Protein: 1 g

Ingredients:

- o 1 sweet potato (6 ounces), peeled, chopped into fries
- o Salt as per taste
- o 1half tsps olive oil
- o A large pinch garlic powder
- o half tsp minced fresh thyme
- o Cooking spray

Directions:

1. For 30 minutes, submerge the diced sweet potatoes in a container of cold water. To dry, drain and use a kitchen towel.

2. Arrange the fries in a bowl and top with oil. Well, toss. Salt, garlic powder, and thyme should be added.

3. Put the sweet potatoes in the basket of the air fryer.

4. Air fried at 400 °F for 14 to 15 minutes, or until golden brown and well cooked.

5. While the basket is frying, shake it a few times.

6. Present hot.

Chapter 4 - Chicken Recipes

Tandoori Chicken

Time needed for prep: 30 minutes

Time needed to cook: 15 minutes

Serves: 2

Nutritional values per serving:

Calories: 178

Fat: 6 g

Carb: 2 g

Fiber Content: 0 g

Total Protein: 25 g

Ingredients:

For the tandoori chicken:

- o half pd chicken tenders, halved
- o 2 cloves garlic, peeled, minced
- o half tbsp fresh ginger, minced
- o quarter cup Yogurt (Greek)
- o half tsp chili powder or cayenne pepper or use lesser according to taste
- o half tsp salt or to taste
- o half tsp turmeric powder
- o A few drops orange food coloring (optional)
- o half tsp garam masala
- o Cooking spray or oil for basting
- o To serve (optional):
- o Lemon wedges to serve
- o A handful fresh cilantro, chopped, to garnish
- o Sliced onions to serve

Directions:

1. Combine the yogurt, garam masala, chili powder, ginger powder, salt, food coloring, and turmeric powder in a bowl.

2. Apply this mixture to the chicken to marinate it. For around 30 minutes, refrigerate.

3. Insert the chicken pieces into the air fryer basket without the marinade.

4. Lightly grease a brush or sprinkle some cooking spray. Spray cooking spray again after flipping the sides.

5. Air fried for 12 minutes at 400 °F in a preheated air fryer. After 6 minutes of cooking, turn the chicken over, adding additional oil as you go.

6. Air-fry the meat until a meat cooking thermometer reads 165 °F for the inside.

7. Present with lemon wedges and thinly sliced onions.

Baked Thai Peanut Chicken Egg Rolls

Time needed for prep: 10 minutes

Time needed to cook: 8 minutes

Serves: 2

Nutritional values per serving:

Calories: 235

Fat: 2 g

Carb: 17 g

Fiber Content: 1 g

Total Protein: 21 g

Ingredients:

- 2 egg roll wrappers
- 2 tbsps Thai peanut sauce
- 2 green onions, chopped
- half cup shredded rotisserie chicken
- 1 small carrot, very thinly sliced

o   ⅛ red peppers, sliced

Directions:

Chicken should be put in a bowl. The chicken should be covered in Thai peanut sauce.

2. Arrange your countertop with the egg roll wrappers. Carrot, onion, and bell pepper should be divided equally and placed on the bottom third of the wrappers. Place the chicken atop the vegetables after dividing it.

3. Use water to dampen the wrappers' edges. Roll the wrappers tightly after slightly folding the sides over the filling. Until you're ready to fry, cover with wet paper towels.

4. Cooking spray should be used liberally to the egg rolls. Put inside the basket of the air fryer.

5. Air-fry at 390 °F for 6 to 8 minutes, or until the food is crisp.

6. Slice in half, then serve with Thai peanut sauce.

Air Fryer Chicken Nuggets

Time needed for prep: 10 minutes

Time needed to cook: 8 minutes

Serves: 2

Nutritional values per serving:

Calories: 200

Fat: 4 g

Carb: 13 g

Fiber Content: 1 g

Total Protein: 26 g

Ingredients:

o   half pd chicken breasts, skinless, boneless, chopped into bite-sized chunks
o   2 tbsps pickle juice or extra buttermilk
o   2 tbsps buttermilk
o   Salt as per taste
o   2 tbsps whole-wheat flour

- o quarter cup bread crumbs (panko)
- o quarter tsp pepper or to taste
- o quarter tsp garlic powder
- o quarter tsp paprika
- o Ketchup to serve
- o Cooking spray

Directions:

1. In a bowl, combine the buttermilk, salt, and pickle juice.

2. Stir in the chicken. Wait for 30 to 40 minutes.

3. Drain the chicken, then put it on a plate.

4. Combine all the ingredients in a ziplock bag. Shake the bag vigorously after sealing it.

5. Fill the bag with chicken and close it. Shake to thoroughly cover the chicken.

6. Use cooking spray to grease the air fryer basket.

7. Air-fry for 8 minutes or until crisp in an air fryer that has been preheated to 400 °F.

8. Serve with ketchup or your preferred dip.

Chick-fil-A Chicken Sandwich

Time needed for prep: 10 minutes

Time needed to cook: 14 minutes

Serves: 3

Nutritional values per serving:

Calories: 281

Fat: 6 g

Carb: 38 g

Fiber Content: 1 g

Total Protein: 15 g

Ingredients:

- 1 chicken breast, skinless, boneless, pded until half inch in thickness
- 1 egg
- half cup flour (all purpose)
- 1 tbsp potato starch
- half tsp sea salt
- quarter tsp garlic powder
- half tbsp extra-virgin olive oil
- 2–3 hamburger buns, toasted, buttered
- quarter cup dill pickle juice
- quarter cup milk
- 1 tbsp powdered sugar
- half tsp paprika
- Ground pepper as per taste
- $\frac{1}{8}$ tsp ground celery seeds
- Dill pickle chips to serve
- Mayonnaise to serve

Directions:

1. Cut the chicken into 2 to 3 pieces.

2. Fill a ziplock bag with chicken and pickle juice before sealing it. A few turns of the bag will ensure that the chicken is thoroughly covered in pickle juice. For 30 to 60 minutes, chill.

3. In a bowl, whisk together the milk and egg.

4. Fill another small bowl with the flour, potato starch, and all the seasonings.

5. Dip chicken into the egg mixture first. Shake to remove any extra egg.

6. Dredge the meat in the flour mixture next. Shake to remove any extra flour. This action is required.

7. Spray cooking spray on the basket of the air fryer. Chicken pieces should be placed in the air fryer basket. Cooking spray should be applied to the chicken.

8. Air fried for 12 minutes at 340 °F in a preheated air fryer. After 6 minutes of cooking, turn the chicken over, adding additional oil as you go.

9. Raise the heat to 400 degrees Fahrenheit. For two minutes, cook. Cook the opposite side for 2 minutes after flipping the sides.

10. Top the bottom half of the hamburger buns with the chicken. Add some mayonnaise on top of it. Serve with cayenne pepper if desired and dill pickle chips.

Chicken Fried Rice

Time needed for prep: 5 minutes

Time needed to cook: 20 minutes

Serves: 3

Nutritional values per serving:

Calories: 420

Fat: 2 g

Carb: 80 g

Fiber Content: 3 g

Total Protein: 15 g

Ingredients:

- o 1half cups cold rice
- o 2half tbsps soy sauce
- o 1 green onion, sliced
- o ¾ cup frozen vegetables of your choice
- o half tsp vegetable oil
- o half tsp sesame oil
- o Salt as per taste

Directions:

1. Combine all of the ingredients in a bowl and stir thoroughly.

2. Insert into the baking accessory for the air fryer.

3. Set up the air fryer with the baking accessories.

4. Air fried for 12 to 15 minutes at 340 °F in a preheated air fryer. Every five minutes, stir.

5. Present heat.

Southwest Chicken Salad

Time needed for prep: 20 minutes

Time needed to cook: 30 minutes

Serves: 2

Nutritional values per serving:

Calories: 271

Fat: 6 g

Carb: 21 g

Fiber Content: 5 g

Total Protein: 29 g

Ingredients:

For chicken:

- half pd boneless, skinless chicken breasts, thawed
- half tbsp avocado oil
- quarter tsp cumin powder
- ⅛ tsp garlic powder
- 1 tbsp lime juice (freshly squeezed)
- quarter tsp chili powder
- ⅛ tsp onion powder
- ⅛ tsp salt or to taste

For salad:

- 2 cups green leaf lettuce
- 1 small avocado
- half cup black beans, drained, rinsed
- half cup corn
- half cup halved cherry tomatoes
- Southwestern dressing or any other dressing of your choice, as required

Directions:

1. Combine the chicken, lime juice, and oil in a bowl. Stirring is necessary to thoroughly coat the chicken with the mixture.

2. Stir in a bowl with all the seasonings. Sprinkle the chicken all over. For 20 to 30 minutes, refrigerate it with a tight cover.

3. Remove the chicken from the marinating marinade and put it in the air fryer basket.

4. Bake for 25 minutes at 400 °F in an air fryer that has been preheated. After baking for 12 to 13 minutes, turn over the sides. Cook the chicken until the internal temperature reaches 165 °F.

5. Place the chicken on the cutting board after removing it from the air fryer. Chop or shred the chicken when it is safe to handle.

6. Fill a bowl with all the salad ingredients. Stir in the chicken well. Add dressing on top, then thoroughly toss.

7. Serve.

Chicken Shawarma Bowl

Time needed for prep: 10 minutes

Time needed to cook: 12–15 minutes

Serves: 2

Nutritional values per serving:

Calories: 313

Fat: 17 g

Carb: 12 g

Fiber Content: 3 g

Total Protein: 29 g

Ingredients:

<u>For chicken shawarma:</u>

- o   half pd chicken thighs, skinless, boneless, chopped into bite-sized pieces
- o   half tsp kosher salt
- o   1 tsp oregano herbs (dry)
- o   half tsp cumin powder
- o   quarter tsp ground allspice
- o   1 tbsp vegetable oil
- o   half tsp cinnamon powder
- o   half tsp coriander powder
- o   For the bowl:
- o   ¾ cup halved grape tomatoes
- o   half small English cucumber, sliced
- o   half cup pitted olives
- o   half cup cooked cauliflower rice

- o   1 cup salad greens
- o   Dry roasted chickpeas to garnish (optional)
- o   For the dressing (optional):
- o   half cup nonfat Yogurt (Greek)
- o   A pinch oregano
- o   1-2 tbsps lime juice

Directions:

1. Combine oregano, salt, and all the other spices in a bowl.

Chicken should be put in a bowl. Pour some oil on it. Add the spice mixture on top and well combine.

3. Leave out for 30 to 60 minutes at room temperature.

4. Insert into the basket of an air fryer.

5. Air-fry at 350 °F for 12 to 15 minutes, or until the food is crisp. Halfway through the frying process, shake the basket.

6. To make the dressing, combine all the ingredients in a bowl and whisk to combine.

7. Grab two serving bowls to assemble. Place salad greens in each bowl. You can arrange the olives, tomatoes, cucumber, chicken shawarma, cauliflower rice, and other ingredients as you choose.

8. If desired, drizzle the yogurt dressing on top. If using, garnish with roasted garbanzo beans before serving.

General Tso Chicken

Time needed for prep: 20 minutes

Time needed to cook: 15 minutes

Serves: 2

Nutritional values per serving:

Calories: 302

Fat: 13 g

Carb: 18 g

Fiber Content: 0 g

Total Protein: 26 g

Ingredients:

For chicken:

- o half pd chicken thighs, skinless, boneless, chopped into chunks
- o 3 tbsps cornflour
- o Salt as per taste
- o White pepper as per taste
- o 1 small egg, well beaten
- o For Tso general sauce:
- o 1 tsp unseasoned rice wine vinegar
- o 1 tsp cornflour
- o 1 tbsp soy sauce
- o 1 tsp sugar
- o 3-4 tbsps chicken stock or broth
- o 1 tbsp ketchup
- o half tbsp garlic, minced
- o half tbsp ginger, minced
- o half tsp sesame oil
- o 1-2 dried whole red chili, deseeded, chopped
- o half tsp toasted sesame seeds
- o 1 tbsp green onion (sliced fine)
- o 1 tsp canola oil

Directions:

1. To prepare chicken, place it in the egg bowl and toss until thoroughly coated.

2. In a shallow bowl, combine cornflour, salt, and pepper. Put some of it on the chicken. Shake the chicken to remove any extra cornstarch.

3. Put the chicken in the basket of the air fryer.

4. Air-fry at 400 °F for 12 to 15 minutes, or until golden brown and well done. Halfway through cooking, flip the chicken.

5. Create the Tso sauce as follows in the interim: In a bowl, combine the cornflour, soy sauce, broth, sugar, ketchup, and vinegar. Whisk thoroughly.

6. Heat a pan to a medium temperature. Heat before adding canola oil. Stir for 4-5 seconds after adding the chiles. Add the ginger and garlic, stir, and cook until fragrant. Stir continuously while adding the cornflour mixture until thick. Add the chicken, then fully heat. Remove from the heat.

7. Stir in half a tablespoon of green onion and sesame oil.

8. Present the chicken with rice. Serve the dish garnished with the leftover green onion and sesame seeds.

Potato Chip Chicken

Time needed for prep: 15 minutes

Time needed to cook: 15 minutes

Serves: 2

Nutritional values per serving:

Calories: 314

Fat: 15 g

Carb: 14 g

Fiber Content: 1 g

Total Protein: 28 g

Ingredients:

- o half pd chicken breasts, thinly sliced
- o 2 ounces potato chips, crushed
- o 1 egg
- o half tsp all-purpose seasoning (optional)

Directions:

1. Use cooking spray that is nonstick to grease the air fryer basket.

2. In a deep, broad dish, beat the egg.

3. Spread out the chip crumbs on a platter.

4. Start by drizzling chicken slices with egg. Shake to remove any extra egg. Dredge in chips next. Place in the air fryer after pressing to adhere.

5. Air-fry at 400 °F for 12 to 15 minutes, or until golden brown and well done. Halfway through cooking, flip the chicken. Additionally, the exterior should be crisp and brown.

Calzones

Time needed for prep: 15 minutes

Time needed to cook: 12 minutes

Serves: 4

Nutritional values per serving:

Calories: 348

Fat: 12 g

Carb: 44 g

Fiber Content: 5 g

Total Protein: 21 g

Ingredients:

- o   2 tsps olive oil
- o   6 ounces spinach leaves (small)
- o   4 ounces shredded rotisserie chicken breast
- o   3 ounces pre-shredded mozzarella
- o   half cup minced red onion
- o   ⅔ cup marinara sauce
- o   12 ounces fresh, prepared whole-wheat pizza dough

Directions:

1. Heat a nonstick pan to a high temperature. oil is added. Once the oil is hot, add the onion and cook it until it is transparent.

2. After adding it, boil the spinach until it wilts. Turn off the heat.

3. Stir in the chicken and marinara sauce.

4. Divide the dough into 8 equal sections. create balls out of.

5. Sprinkle some flour on your countertop. Make circles out of the dough balls that are 6 inches in diameter.

6. Place the chicken mixture on one side of the circle after dividing it among the rolled pieces of dough. Over the filling, secure the second half. To seal, crimp the edges.

7. Use cooking spray to coat the calzones before placing them in the air fryer.

8. Bake for 12 to 15 minutes, or until golden brown, in an air fryer that has been preheated to 350 °F. About halfway through baking, turn the calzones.

9. Allow to cool before serving.

Chicken Wings

Time needed for prep: 10 minutes

Time needed to cook: 30 minutes

Serves: 1

Nutritional values per serving:

Calories: 304

Fat: 19 g

Carb: 8 g

Fiber Content: 0 g

Total Protein: 23 g

Ingredients:

- o 5 chicken drumettes
- o 1half tsps soy sauce
- o 1 tsp honey
- o half tsp crushed garlic
- o 1 tsp lime juice or to taste
- o Red pepper flakes to taste (optional if you want it spicier)
- o quarter tsp minced ginger
- o half tsp sambal oelek (ground fresh chili paste)
- o Sliced scallions to garnish
- o Kosher salt as per taste
- o Cooking spray

Directions:

1. Use cooking spray to coat the chicken. Chicken should be put in the air fryer basket.

2. Air-fry for roughly 25 minutes at 400 °F in a preheated air fryer.

3. While the chicken is cooking, turn the drumettes about 2-3 times.

4. In a saucepan, combine the sambal oelek, honey, soy sauce, cornflour, red pepper flakes, ginger, garlic, salt, and lime juice. Stirring continuously, place the saucepan over the heat and bring to a boil for two to three minutes.

5. Add the chicken and stir to thoroughly coat.

6. Place in a serving dish. Serve with lime juice, chives, scallions, and cilantro.

Spicy Chicken Thighs

Time needed for prep: 6–8 hours

Time needed to cook: 16 minutes

Serves: 2

Nutritional values per serving:

Calories: 458

Fat: 13 g

Carb: 36 g

Fiber Content: 4 g

Total Protein: 52 g

Ingredients:

For marinating chicken:

- o 1 cup low-fat buttermilk
- o quarter tsp cayenne pepper
- o half tsp paprika
- o 2 chicken thighs, boneless, skinless
- o half cup flour (all purpose)
- o 1 tbsp water
- o quarter tsp kosher salt or to taste
- o 1 egg
- o 1 cup bread crumbs (panko)
- o Hot sauce to serve
- o Cooking spray

Directions:

1. To marinate chicken, combine all of the marinating ingredients in a basin and stir thoroughly. For 6 to 8 hours, place it in the refrigerator with a tight cover.

2. Take the marinated chicken out and arrange it on a plate. Throw away the marinade mixture.

3. Fill a small basin with salt and flour.

4. Put panko (bread crumbs) in a another bowl.

5. In a third bowl, thoroughly mix the egg and water.

6. First, coat the chicken with the flour mixture. Then, cover it with egg mixture. Shake to remove any extra egg, then roll it in the bread crumbs. Chicken should be put in the air fryer basket.

7. Air-fry at 400 °F for 16 minutes, or until crisp, golden brown, and well cooked. After 8 minutes of cooking, flip the sides.

8. Before serving, drizzle some hot sauce over the chicken thighs.

Ranch Chicken Tenders

Time needed for prep: 5 minutes

Time needed to cook: 12 minutes

Serves: 2

Nutritional values per serving: (2 chicken tenders):

Calories: 197

Fat: 4 g

Carb: 12 g

Fiber Content: 1 g

Total Protein: 25 g

Ingredients:

- o 4 chicken tenders
- o 1 tbsp water
- o 1 egg
- o 1 cup bread crumbs (panko)
- o Hot sauce to serve
- o Cooking spray

For ranch seasoning:

- o quarter tsp salt or to taste
- o quarter tsp garlic powder
- o ⅛ tsp paprika
- o ⅛ tsp pepper or to taste
- o quarter tsp onion powder
- o half tsp dried parsley

Directions:

1. Place all of the ranch seasoning's components in a small bowl and whisk.

2. Put panko (bread crumbs) in a another bowl.

3. In a third bowl, thoroughly mix the egg and water.

4. Season the chicken with ranch dressing. Then, cover it with egg mixture. Shake to remove any extra egg, then roll it in the bread crumbs. Chicken should be put in the air fryer basket. Cooking spray should be applied to the chicken.

5. Air-fry at 400 °F for 12 minutes, or until crisp, golden brown, and well cooked. After 6 minutes of cooking, flip the sides. After flipping the sides, spray some cooking spray.

6. Present hot.

Chapter 5 - Beef Recipes

Roast Beef

Time needed for prep: 5 minutes

Time needed to cook: 30 minutes

Serves: 3

Nutritional values per serving:

Calories: 293

Fat: 19 g

Carb: 0 g

Fiber Content: 0 g

Total Protein: 29 g

Ingredients:

- o 1 pd rump roast
- o Fresh pepper powder
- o half tsp salt
- o half tsp rosemary
- o half tbsp olive oil

Directions:

1. In a bowl, combine the salt, rosemary, and oil. Rub the mixture all over the beef. To marinate, set away for some time.

2. Cover the air fryer basket's bottom with aluminum foil.

3. Take the roast out of the air fryer and put it in the basket.

4. Depending on how you prefer it cooked, air-fry at 360 °F for 30 to 40 minutes in a preheated air fryer.

5. Take out and set on your cutting board after air fryer. Wrap it in foil. Give it a few minutes' separation. Slice the meat and serve it with your preferred gravy or sauce, as well as roasted or steam veggies, etc.

Beef Empanadas

Time needed for prep: 30 minutes

Time needed to cook: 7 minutes

Serves: 1

Nutritional values per serving: (4 empanadas):

Calories: 343

Fat: 19 g

Carb: 25 g

Fiber Content: 2 g

Total Protein: 17 g

Ingredients:

- 1.5 ounces ground beef
- half tbsp olive oil
- half small onion, minced
- 1 large clove garlic, peeled, minced
- $\frac{1}{8}$ tsp paprika
- A pinch cinnamon powder
- quarter cup tomatoes (chopped)
- 1.5 ounces chopped cremini mushrooms
- 3 pitted green olives, sliced
- 1 egg, beaten
- 4 square gyoza wrappers
- $\frac{1}{8}$ tsp cumin powder
- Salt as per taste
- Pepper as per taste

Directions:

1. Heat a pan to a high temperature. Oil is then heated. Sauté the steak, onion, and seasoning until light brown. As it cooks, break it simultaneously. Any surplus fat that is still in the pan should be discarded.

2. Stir in the mushrooms and garlic. Cook it for two to three minutes with a lid on.

3. Stir in cumin, cinnamon, paprika, olives, salt, and pepper. Cook the mushrooms until they are soft. Mix thoroughly after adding tomatoes. For one minute, cook. Turn off the heat. Wait 10 minutes for it to cool.

4. Arrange your countertop with the gyoza wrappers.

5. In the middle of the wrapper, spread roughly 1 1/2 tbsp of the meat mixture. Apply the egg mixture to the borders. The second half should be folded over the meat and the edges pressed together to seal.

6. Apply the remaining egg mixture all over the empanada.

7. Fry for about 7 minutes, or until crisp and browned, in an air fryer that has been preheated to 400 °F.

8. Serve.

Easy Spring Rolls

Time needed for prep: 20 minutes

Time needed to cook: 15-16 minutes

Serves:

Nutritional values per serving:

Calories: 112

Fat: 3.2 g

Carb: 16.4 g

Fiber Content: 0.7 g

Total Protein: 4.1 g

Ingredients:

- o   1 ounce dried rice noodles
- o   3.5 ounces ground beef
- o   half small onion, diced
- o   half tsp soy sauce
- o   half vegetable oil
- o   half sesame oil
- o   half cup frozen mixed vegetable
- o   2 cloves garlic, crushed
- o   8 ounces egg roll wrappers

Directions:

Noodles should be placed in a bowl of hot water. After five minutes, drain. Noodles should be cut into smaller pieces.

2. Heat a wok to a medium-high temperature. Include sesame oil. Add the steak, onion, mixed veggies, and garlic after the oil is hot. Brown the beef in the pan. Turn off the heat.

3. Stir in the noodles. Put it to the side for a while. Then, stir in the soy sauce.

4. Set egg roll wrappers out on your counter. Diagonally position some filler. Across the filling, fold the top corner. Overlap the filling with the side corners. The final bend should be wetted. Place the spring rolls in the air fryer with their seam side facing down after rolling them up and pressing the final corner to adhere. Cook in groups.

5. Apply vegetable oil to the spring rolls.

6. Cook in an air fryer that has been preheated to 400 °F for about 7-8 minutes, or until crisp.

7. Serve.

Meat Loaf

Time needed for prep: 10 minutes

Time needed to cook: 25 -30 minutes

Serves: 8

Nutritional values per serving:

Calories: 297

Fat: 18.8 g

Carb: 5.9 g

Fiber Content: 0.8 g

Total Protein: 24.8 g

Ingredients:

- o 2 pds lean ground beef
- o 6 tbsps dry bread crumbs
- o 2 tbsps chopped fresh thyme
- o 1half tsps freshly pepper powder powder
- o 4 mushrooms, chop into thick slices
- o 2 eggs, lightly beaten
- o 1 chopped onion, chopped
- o 2 tsps salt or to taste
- o A little olive oil to brush

Directions:

1. Place everything on the ingredient list in a bowl, excluding the mushrooms. Use your hands to thoroughly blend the mixture.

2. Spoon the mixture into a bread pan that will fit easily inside an air fryer or a baking attachment for an air fryer. Smoothly and evenly spread the mixture.

3. Lay sliced mushrooms on top of the meat and lightly push them into the meat.

4. Apply olive oil to the top.

5. Bake for about 25 minutes, or until brown, in an air fryer that has been preheated to 390 °F.

6. Remove from the air fryer and allow to cool for ten to twelve minutes.

7. Slice and serve with fried potatoes and your preferred salad.

Mock Taco Bell Crunch Wraps

Time needed for prep: 15 minutes

Time needed to cook: 4 minutes

Serves: 3

Nutritional values per serving:

Calories: 954

Fat: 30 g

Carb: 34 g

Fiber Content: 2 g

Total Protein: 42 g

Ingredients:

- o   1 pd ground beef
- o   ⅔ cup water
- o   3 small Roma tomatoes
- o   1 cup chopped lettuce
- o   1 cup sour cream
- o   Taco seasoning to taste
- o   3 flour tortillas (12 inches each)
- o   6 ounces nacho cheese
- o   1 cup Mexican blend cheese
- o   3 tostadas

Directions:

1. Place a skillet over medium heat. Once beef is added, brown it. As it cooks, break it simultaneously. Turn off the heat. The remaining fat in the pan should be drained.

2. Stir in the taco seasoning. For 1-2 minutes, cook. Turn off the heat.

3. Arrange your tortillas on the counter. Between the tortillas, distribute the beef.

4. Top the meat with the nacho cheese. Put a tostada on every one. Over the nacho cheese layer, evenly distribute the sour cream, lettuce, tomatoes, and cheese.

5. Wrap the food firmly and put it in the air fryer basket seam side down.

6. Use cooking spray on the wraps. Cook in batches as necessary.

7. Air-fry for roughly 2 minutes at 350 °F in a preheated air fryer. After two minutes of frying, flip the sides.

Air Fryer Steak

Time needed for prep: 5 minutes

Time needed to cook: 12 minutes

Serves: 6

Nutritional values per serving: (4 ounces):

Calories: 250

Fat: 17 g

Carb: 0 g

Fiber Content: 0 g

Total Protein: 23 g

Ingredients:

- o 2 New York strip steak or rib eye steak (12 ounces each, 1 inch in thickness)
- o Salt as per taste
- o Paprika to taste (optional)
- o Pepper as per taste
- o 1 tsp garlic powder or to taste (optional)
- o Butter to serve

Directions:

1. Season the steaks with salt, pepper, paprika, and garlic powder. Put inside the basket of the air fryer.

2. Grill for 12 minutes or to the desired doneness in an air fryer that has been preheated to 400° F. Halfway through frying, flip the sides. If necessary, cook in batches. each into three equal pieces.

3. Add butter to the dish.

Air-Fried Taco Dogs

Time needed for prep: 5 minutes

Time needed to cook: 10 minutes

Serves: 1

Nutritional values per serving:

Calories: 418

Fat: 28 g

Carb: 28.7 g

Fiber Content: 3 g

Total Protein: 14 g

Ingredients:

- o 1 jumbo hot dog
- o 1 hot dog bun
- o 2 tbsps salsa
- o half tsp taco seasoning mix
- o 2–3 tbsps guacamole
- o 3 pickled jalapeño slices

Directions:

1. Slit the hot dog four or five times. Taco seasoning should be sprinkled over the hot dog and thoroughly rubbed in.

2. Put in the basket of the air fryer.

3. Air-fry for 5 minutes at 320 °F in an air fryer that has been preheated.

4. Cut a slit down the length of the hot dog bun, but stop short of the bottom (as shown in the picture).

5. Insert the bun into the air fryer and insert the hot dog into the slit.

6. Cook until crisp, about 3 to 4 minutes.

7. Sprinkle jalapenos on top of the hot dog. Serve with salsa and guacamole.

Air Fryer Steak Tips

Time needed for prep: 5 minutes

Time needed to cook: 9 minutes

Serves: 6

Nutritional values per serving:

Calories: 526

Fat: 34 g

Carb: 6 g

Fiber Content: 3 g

Total Protein: 49 g

Ingredients:

- o 3 pds steak
- o 2 tsps oil
- o 1 tsp ground pepper
- o 1 tsp onion powder
- o 1 tsp salt
- o 1 tsp garlic powder
- o quarter tsp cayenne pepper
- o For asparagus:
- o 2 pds asparagus, trimmed
- o 1 tsp oil (optional)
- o half tsp salt

Directions:

1. Place all of the marinade ingredients in a bowl. Mix thoroughly. Stir in the steak well. the meat chunks with the mixture thoroughly.

2. Spray cooking spray in the basket of the air fryer. Make batches of food.

3. Depending on how you prefer it done, air-fry for 4-6 minutes at 400 °F in a preheated air fryer. Take out and keep heated after using the air fryer.

4. Season the asparagus with salt and oil, then toss well.

5. After putting the asparagus in the air fryer basket, heat it for three minutes.

6. Combine asparagus and steak tips.

Cheeseburgers

Time needed for prep: 5 minutes

Time needed to cook: 15 minutes

Serves: 2

Nutritional values per serving:

Calories: 524

Fat: 32 g

Net Carb: 22 g

Fiber Content: 0 g

Total Protein: 30 g

Ingredients:

- o   half pd 80% lean ground chuck beef
- o   half tsp Worcestershire sauce
- o   Salt as per taste
- o   Pepper as per taste
- o   2 burger buns, split, lightly toasted if desired
- o   2 cheese slices
- o   half tsp liquid smoke
- o   2 tsps burger seasoning
- o   Mayonnaise (optional)
- o   Toppings of your choice like lettuce, tomato slices, etc. (optional)
- o   Cooking spray

Directions:

1. In a bowl, combine the ground beef, seasoning, salt, pepper, Worcestershire sauce, and liquid smoke.

2. Divide the mixture into two equal halves, then form each into a patty.

3. Spray cooking spray in the basket of the air fryer. Burgers should be put in the air fryer basket.

4. Grill for 12 minutes or to the desired doneness in an air fryer that has been preheated to 360 oF. Halfway through grilling, flip the sides.

5. Top each hamburger with a slice of cheese.

Put in the air fryer at step 6. Until the cheese melts, grill for one minute.

7. Arrange a burger on each bun's bottom half. If using, spread mayonnaise on the cut-off portion of the buns. Insert toppings. After serving, top with the remaining buns.

Steak and Mushrooms

Time needed for prep: 4–8 hours

Time needed to cook: 10 minutes

Serves: 2

Nutritional values per serving:

Calories: 225

Fat: 13.2 g

Carb: 5.8 g

Fiber Content: 0.9 g

Total Protein: 20.8 g

Ingredients:

- o   half pd beef sirloin steak, chop into bite-sized cubes
- o   2 tbsps Worcestershire sauce
- o   half tsp parsley flakes
- o   half tsp crushed chili flakes
- o   4 ounces button mushrooms, sliced
- o   half tbsp olive oil
- o   half tsp paprika

Directions:

1. Combine all of the listed ingredients in a bowl.

2. For 4 to 8 hours, cover and chill. 30 minutes prior to using the air fryer, remove the bowl from the refrigerator.

3. Using a spoon, remove the steak and mushrooms and put them in the air fryer basket. Throw away the marinade.

4. Depending on how you prefer it done, air fried for 9 to 10 minutes at 400 °F in a preheated air fryer. About halfway through cooking, shake the basket.

5. Allow it to cool for five minutes prior to serving.

Chapter 6 - Pork Recipes

Easy Air Fryer Pork Chops

Time needed for prep: 5 minutes

Time needed to cook: 10 minutes

Serves: 4

Nutritional values per serving:

Calories: 247

Fat: 13 g

Carb: 1 g

Fiber Content: 0 g

Total Protein: 29 g

Ingredients:

- o   4 pork chops of 1 inch in thickness (with or without bone)
- o   1half tsps minced fresh rosemary
- o   1 tsp lemon zest (grated)
- o   half tsp onion powder
- o   half tsp pepper
- o   1 tsp paprika
- o   half tsp garlic powder
- o   half tsp salt or to taste
- o   quarter tsp crushed red pepper
- o   Olive oil, as required
- o   Cooking spray

Directions:

1. Give the pork chops a thorough oiling. Rub it in thoroughly.

2. Combine all of the remaining ingredients in a bowl. The chops should be well-rubbed with this mixture.

3. Use cooking spray to grease the air fryer basket.

4. Arrange the pork chops in a single layer in the air fryer basket. A small space should exist between the pork chops. Whenever required, cook in batches.

5. Fry for 10-13 minutes, or until the desired doneness, in an air fryer that has been preheated to 400 °F.

6. Serve immediately.

Breaded Pork Chops

Time needed for prep: 10 minutes

Time needed to cook: 12 minutes

Serves: 2

Nutritional values per serving:

Calories: 376

Fat: 8.9 g

Carb: 28 g

Fiber Content: 2.8 g

Total Protein: 43.9 g

Ingredients:

- o 2 lean and trimmed pork chops
- o 2 tbsps water
- o 2 tsps paprika
- o quarter tsp garlic powder
- o quarter tsp cayenne pepper or to taste
- o quarter tsp salt or to taste
- o 1 small egg, beaten
- o half cup bread crumbs (panko)

- o   1 tsp oregano herbs (dry)
- o   1 tsp pepper
- o   half tsp dry mustard
- o   Cooking spray
- o   To serve (optional):
- o   Steamed vegetables
- o   Cauliflower rice
- o   Salad

Directions:

1. Combine salt, spices, and bread crumbs (panko) in a bowl and whisk.

2. In a separate bowl, mix together the egg and the water.

3. Submerge the pork in the egg mixture first. Shake to remove any extra egg.

4. After that, roll it in the mixture of bread crumbs. Put the pork in the basket of the air fryer. Cooking spray should be used on the chops.

5. Fry for 12 minutes at 380 °F in a preheated air fryer, or until crisp, golden brown, and well cooked. After 8 minutes of cooking, flip the chops. After rotating the pork chops, spray once more. When the meat reaches a temperature of 145 °F, the chops are said to be done.

6. Remove the food from the air fryer and allow it to cool for three minutes.

7. If preferred, serve with suggested serving choices.

Pork Dumplings with Dipping Sauce

Time needed for prep: 30 minutes

Time needed to cook: 12 minutes

Serves: 3

Nutritional values per serving:

Calories: 140

Fat: 5 g

Carb: 16 g

Fiber Content: 1 g

Total Protein: 7 g

Ingredients:

- half tsp canola oil
- half tbsp minced fresh ginger
- 2 ounces ground pork
- 9 dumpling wrappers or wonton wrappers (3half inches square)
- 1 tbsp rice vinegar
- half tsp toasted sesame oil
- half tbsp chopped scallion
- 2 cups chopped bok choy
- half tbsps crushed garlic
- ⅛ tsp chopped red pepper
- 1 tsp soy sauce (low-sodium)
- quarter tsp packed light brown sugar
- Cooking spray

Directions:

1. Heat a nonstick skillet to a temperature of medium-high. oil is added. Bok choy should be added to hot oil and cooked until it wilts and most of the moisture has disappeared.

2. Add the ginger and garlic and stir until fragrant, about 50 to 60 seconds. Turn off the heat.

3. Use paper towels to pat the mixture dry. Incorporate into a bowl.

4. Place pork and red pepper flakes in the bok choy bowl. Mix thoroughly.

5. Scatter the wonton wrappers around your counter. Each wrapper should have about a tbsp of filling in the center. Water should be delicately brushed along the wrappers' edges. Fold so that you end up with a semicircle. Completely pressing it will seal the edges.

6. Spray cooking spray in the basket of the air fryer.

7. Set the air fryer to cook the dumplings. Avoid crowding them. If necessary, cook in batches. When arranging the dumplings, leave some space between them.

8. Fry for 12 minutes at 375 °F in a preheated air fryer, or until crisp and golden brown. After 6 minutes of cooking, flip the sides.

9. To make the dip, combine the ingredients in a bowl and stir until the sugar is completely dissolved.

10. Serve sauce with the dumplings.

Herb-Crusted Pork Chops

Time needed for prep: 5 minutes

Time needed to cook: 15 minutes

Serves: 2

Nutritional values per serving:

Calories: 194

Fat: 9 g

Carb: 2 g

Fiber Content: 1 g

Total Protein: 24 g

Ingredients:

- half pd pork loin chops, bone-in
- half tbsp herb and garlic seasoning
- half tsp olive oil

Directions:

1. Give the pork chops a thorough oiling. Seasoning should be sprinkled and thoroughly rubbed into the chops.

2. Spray cooking spray in the basket of the air fryer.

3. Fry for 12 minutes at 350 °F in an air fryer that has been preheated. After 6 minutes of cooking, flip the sides.

4. Remove from air fryer and allow to cool for five minutes.

5. Serve.

Air-Fried Bacon

Time needed for prep: 2 minutes

Time needed to cook: 8-10 minutes

Serves: 2

Nutritional values per serving:

Calories: 91

Fat: 8 g

Carb: 0 g

Fiber Content: 0 g

Total Protein: 2 g

Ingredients:

- o   2 slices bacon

Directions:

1. Put the bacon slices in the basket of the air fryer.

2. Air-fry at 400 °F for 8 to 10 minutes, or until the desired doneness, in an air fryer that has been preheated. After 4-5 minutes of frying, flip the sides.

Korean Grilled Pork Dae Ji Bulgogi

Time needed for prep: 40 minutes

Time needed to cook: 15 minutes

Serves: 2

Nutritional values per serving:

Calories: 226

Fat: 8 g

Carb: 8 g

Fiber Content: 0 g

Total Protein: 27 g

Ingredients:

- o   half pd boneless pork shoulder, chop into half-inch-thick cubes
- o   1 tbsp gochujang (Korean red pepper paste)
- o   half tbsp crushed garlic

- half tbsp minced ginger
- 1 onion (sliced)
- half tbsp soy sauce
- half tbsp sesame oil
- Gochugaru or cayenne pepper as per taste
- 1 green onion, thinly sliced
- half tbsp rice wine
- half tsp sugar
- half tbsp sesame seeds

Directions:

1. Combine all of the listed ingredients in a bowl. For one to twenty-four hours, refrigerate it with a tight cover.

30 minutes prior to cooking, remove from the air fryer.

3. Air-fry at 400 °F for 10 to 15 minutes, or until the desired doneness, in an air fryer that has been preheated. After 4-5 minutes of frying, flip the sides.

Raspberry Balsamic Smoked Pork Chops

Time needed for prep: 15 minutes

Time needed to cook: 15 minutes

Serves: 2

Nutritional values per serving:

Calories: 579

Fat: 36 g

Carb: 36 g

Fiber Content: 3 g

Total Protein: 32 g

Ingredients:

- 1 egg
- half cup bread crumbs (panko)
- 2 smoked bone-in pork chops (7–8 ounces each)
- 3 tbsps balsamic vinegar

- o   1 tbsp seedless raspberry jam
- o   2 tbsps 2% milk
- o   half cup chopped pecans
- o   2 tbsps flour (all purpose)
- o   1 tbsp brown sugar
- o   half tbsp thawed frozen orange juice concentrate

Directions:

Spray the air fryer basket with cooking spray liberally in step 1.

2. Pour milk and egg into a small bowl. Stir thoroughly.

3. In a different small bowl, combine pecans and bread crumbs. Stir thoroughly to mix.

4. Fill the third bowl with flour.

5. Initially, coat the pork chops with flour. Shake to release additional flour.

6. After that, add the egg bowl. Apply a thick layer of coating. Shake to scatter a second egg.

7. Dredge in the breadcrumb mixture lastly, and then put the food in the air fryer basket. Avoid overlapping. If necessary, cook in batches.

8. Coat the pork chops with frying spray.

9. Air-fry at 400 °F for 12 to 15 minutes, or until thoroughly cooked and exteriorly golden brown. After cooking for 6-7 minutes, flip the sides. After flipping the pork chops, spray some oil on them.

10. In the meantime, combine orange juice concentrate, brown sugar, raspberry jam, and vinegar in a small pot. Put the pan on the stovetop.

11. Cook, stirring regularly, until just little thick.

12. Place chops on top.

Pork Chops and Broccoli

Time needed for prep: 5 minutes

Time needed to cook: 10 minutes

Serves: 4

Nutritional values per serving:

Calories: 483

Fat: 30 g

Carb: 12 g

Fiber Content: 6 g

Total Protein: 40 g

Ingredients:

- o 4 bone-in pork chops (5 ounces each)
- o 1 tsp paprika
- o 1 tsp garlic powder
- o 1 tsp onion powder
- o 2 tsps salt, divided
- o 4 tbsps avocado oil, divided
- o 4 cloves garlic, minced
- o 4 cups broccoli florets
- o Cooking spray

Directions:

1. Spray cooking spray in the basket of the air fryer.

2. Rub the pork chops with 2 tablespoons of oil. Over the pork chops, liberally season with 1 tsp. salt, paprika, garlic powder, and onion powder. If necessary, cook in batches.

3. Air-fry for five minutes at 350 °F in a preheated air fryer.

4. In the meantime, combine broccoli with 2 tbsps oil, 1 tsp salt, and 1 clove of garlic in a bowl.

5. Turn the pork chops over when the required amount of cooking time has passed. Cover the pork chops with broccoli.

Cook for an additional five minutes. After cooking for 2 to 3 minutes, turn the broccoli.

7. If wanted, serve hot with rice.

Pork Chops with Brussels Sprouts

Time needed for prep: 5 minutes

Time needed to cook: 25 minutes

Serves: 2

Nutritional values per serving:

Calories: 337

Fat: 11 g

Carb: 21 g

Fiber Content: 10 g

Total Protein: 40 g

Ingredients:

- 2 pork chops, bone-in center-cut
- quarter tsp kosher salt
- 2 tsps olive oil
- 2 tsps Dijon mustard
- 1 tsp pepper, divided
- 2 tsps pure maple syrup
- 12 ounces Brussels sprouts, quartered
- Cooking spray

Directions:

1. Coat the pork chops with frying spray. Add a pinch of salt and a teaspoon of pepper.

2. Combine all the ingredients in a bowl, excluding the Brussels sprouts, and whisk well.

3. Stir in the Brussels sprouts.

4. Put the pork chops in the basket of the air fryer. Put the pork chops next to the brussels sprouts. Whenever required, cook in batches.

5. Roast for 10–13 minutes, or to desired doneness, in an air fryer that has been preheated to 400 °F.

Chapter 7 - Lamb Recipes

Greek Lamb and Spinach Meatballs with Tzatziki

Time needed for prep: 20 minutes

Time needed to cook: 11 minutes

Serves: 5 (3 meatballs each)

Nutritional values per serving: NA

Ingredients:

For meatballs:

- ¾ pd ground lamb
- 1 clove crushed garlic
- 3 tbsps chopped pine nuts
- 1 tbsp olive oil
- quarter cup finely crumbled feta
- 1 cup packed chopped spinach
- half cup minced onion
- 1 small egg
- half tbsp minced fresh oregano
- quarter tsp salt or to taste

For Tzatziki:

- half cup Yogurt (Greek)
- 1 tbsp chopped fresh dill
- 1 tsp lime juice
- 1 clove garlic, minced
- 3 tbsps diced cucumber
- 1 tbsp chopped fresh mint
- half tsp olive oil
- Salt as per taste

Directions:

1. Heat a heavy-bottomed pan on the stovetop. oil is added. When the oil is hot enough, add the onion and cook it until it turns brown.

2. Add the garlic and stir until fragrant.

3. Add the spinach and stir; cook until somewhat dry and wilted. Turn off the heat. Incorporate into a bowl.

4. Combine the salt, feta, pine nuts, oregano, and ground lamb thoroughly.

5. Divide the mixture into 15 equal sections and roll each portion into a ball.

6. Bake for 11 minutes in an air fryer that has been preheated to 325 °F, or until fully cooked and gently browned on the outside.

7. In the meantime, combine all of the tzatziki's components in a bowl and stir to combine.

8. Serve the meatballs with your choice of salad and tzatziki.

Lamb Chops with Garlic Sauce

Time needed for prep: 15 minutes

Time needed to cook: 22 minutes

Serves: 2

Nutritional values per serving: NA

Ingredients:

- o 1 small garlic bulb
- o half tbsp fresh oregano, minced
- o 4 lamb chops
- o Ground pepper as per taste
- o 1half tbsps olive oil
- o Salt as per taste

Directions:

1. Rub the garlic bulb with olive oil all over.

2. Put the air fryer basket with the garlic bulb inside.

3. Roast for 12 minutes at 390 °F in an air fryer that has been preheated. Take the finished item out of the basket.

4. Combine oil, oregano, salt, and pepper. The lamb chops should be covered with this mixture. Wait for 5 to 7 minutes. Set the leftover mixture aside.

5. Put the lamb chops in the basket of the air fryer.

6. Roast for 7 minutes at 390 °F in an air fryer that has been preheated.

7. Squeeze the garlic cloves and add them to the remaining oil mixture to produce garlic sauce. Season with salt and pepper. Mix thoroughly.

8. Spoon garlic sauce over the lamb chops. It might go well with couscous.

Lamb Roast with Potatoes, Carrots, and Sweet Potatoes

Time needed for prep: 10 minutes

Time needed to cook: 45 minutes

Serves: 3

Nutritional values per serving: NA

Ingredients:

- o 1.65 pds lamb leg
- o 1 medium sweet potato, peeled, chopped into chunks
- o 4.4 ounces baby carrots
- o pds red royale potatoes, chopped into chunks
- o large cloves garlic, sliced
- o Salt as per taste
- o Pepper as per taste
- o half cup frozen peas, thawed, cooked
- o Olive oil, as required
- o 1 tsp butter
- o 1 large sprig rosemary, sliced

Directions:

1. Slit the lamb all over. Place rosemary and garlic slices into the incisions. Place aside.

2. Wrap the carrots in foil. Place in the baking attachment for an air fryer. Also add the potatoes to the baking tool. Add salt and pepper to taste. Give the potatoes a light oil drizzle and give them a good spin.

3. Put the baking accessory in an air fryer that has been preheated, and roast it at 350 °F for 10 to 15 minutes, or until it is cooked. Take the finished product out of the air fryer and place it somewhere warm.

4. Cover the baking sheet with baking paper, then spread a sheet of aluminum foil over it. Place the sweet potato and lamb on top of it.

5. Roast for 20 to 25 minutes in the air fryer at 350 °F. Lamb should be taken out of the air fryer and put on a cutting board. Wrap it in foil. Give it some time to relax. Slice the lamb once it has cooled enough to handle.

6. If the sweet potato is not fully cooked, roast it for a few more minutes.

7. Arrange baked potatoes, sweet potatoes, carrots, and boiled peas alongside the lamb.

Classic Rack of Lamb (Herbs)

Time needed for prep: 5 minutes

Time needed to cook: 10-12 minutes

Serves: 2

Nutritional values per serving: NA

Ingredients:

- o 1 rack of lamb with 7-8 ribs
- o 3 tsps dried thyme
- o 3-4 tsps dried rosemary
- o 1half tsps crushed garlic
- o quarter cup olive oil
- o half tsp salt
- o half tsp pepper

Directions:

1. Combine the herbs, oil, garlic, salt, and pepper in a bowl.

2. Apply this concoction to the lamb. Put it in the air fryer basket after giving it a thorough rubdown.

3. Depending on the level of doneness required, roast for 10 to 12 minutes in the air fryer at 360 °F.

4. The internal temperature of the meat should be 145 °F if you desire rare, 160 °F if you prefer medium, and 170 °F if you prefer well-done.

Roast Lamb Rack with Lemon and Cumin Crust

Time needed for prep: 15 minutes

Time needed to cook: 25-30 minutes

Serves: 2

Nutritional values per serving:

Ingredients:

- o 0.88 pd Frenched rack of lamb
- o 1 ounce dry bread crumbs
- o quarter tsp salt
- o half tsp cumin seeds
- o quarter tsp grated lemon rind
- o Salt as per taste
- o Ground pepper as per taste
- o half tsp grated garlic
- o half tsp cumin powder
- o 1 small egg, beaten
- o half tsp oil
- o Cooking spray

Directions:

1. Season the rack with salt and pepper.

2. In a shallow bowl, combine the garlic, bread crumbs, lemon zest, oil, salt, cumin seeds, and cumin powder.

3. Next, apply an egg wash to the lamb.

4. After that, roll it in the mixture of bread crumbs. Put the lamb in the basket of the air fryer. Cooking spray should be used on the chops.

5. Cook in an air fryer that has been preheated to 220 °F for 20 minutes or until well done.

6. Increase the heat to 390 °F and cook the food for five minutes.

7. Remove from the air fryer, then wrap in foil. Give it 10 to 12 minutes to relax.

8. Place over your preferred salad.

Spicy Lamb Sirloin Steak

Time needed for prep: 40 minutes

Time needed to cook: 15 minutes

Serves: 2

Nutritional values per serving:

Calories: 182

Fat: 7 g

Carb: 3 g

Fiber Content: 1 g

Total Protein: 24 g

Ingredients:

- quarter cup chopped onion
- 3 cloves garlic, peeled
- half tsp ground fennel
- quarter tsp ground cardamom
- half tsp salt
- 2 slices ginger
- half tsp garam masala
- half tsp cinnamon powder
- Cayenne pepper as per taste
- half pd lamb sirloin steaks, boneless

Directions:

1. Remove the lamb steak from the equation and combine the components in a blender. Once the onion is chopped, blend.

2. Cut the lamb steak into a few little slits. The lamb chops should be covered with the mixed mixture. For one to twenty-four hours, refrigerate it with a tight cover. The lamb chops should be taken out of the refrigerator 30 minutes prior to cooking.

3. For 12 minutes, preheat the air fryer at 330 °F.

4. Set the air fryer to cook lamb steaks.

5. Cook for 10 to 15 minutes, or until the desired degree of doneness. Halfway through cooking, flip the sides. For medium-rare, the internal temperature of the meat should be 150 °F.

Braised Lamb Shanks

Time needed for prep: 5 minutes

Time needed to cook: 1half–2 hours

Serves: 2

Nutritional values per serving:

Calories: 447

Fat: 26 g

Carb: 6 g

Fiber Content: 2 g

Total Protein: 24 g

Ingredients:

- o 2 lamb shanks
- o Ground pepper as per taste
- o Kosher salt as per taste
- o 1 tbsp olive oil
- o 2 cloves garlic, crushed
- o 1half cups beef broth, divided
- o 2–3 sprigs fresh rosemary
- o 1 tbsp balsamic vinegar

Directions:

1. Add salt and pepper to the lamb shanks. Rub it in thoroughly.

2. Put the lamb in the baking accessory for the air fryer.

3. Rub the meat with oil. Around and beneath the lamb, scatter thyme.

4. Insert in air fryer.

5. Roast for 20 minutes at 425 °F in an air fryer that has been preheated.

6. Reduce the heat to 250 °F. Around the meat, pour vinegar and 1 cup of broth. For two hours, cook. After simmering for an hour, pour any leftover broth.

7. The flesh is done when the bone starts to fall off.

Brussels Sprouts and Potato Quenelles

Time needed for prep: 15 minutes

Time needed to cook: 2 hours

Serves: 2

Nutritional values per serving:

Ingredients:

- pds leg of lamb
- 2-3 sprigs lemon thyme
- 2-3 sprigs rosemary
- 1 tsp groundnut oil
- 10.5 ounces Brussels sprouts
- 1 small clove garlic
- 1-2 tbsps honey
- 1-2 tbsps olive oil
- For quenelles:
- large boiled potatoes
- 1 pinch nutmeg
- 1-2 tbsps warm milk
- 1 tbsp butter
- Salt as per taste
- Pepper as per taste

Directions:

1. Cut a few slits into the lamb all throughout. Fill the slits with thyme and rosemary.

2. Use peanut oil to brush.

3. Cook for 75 minutes at 150 °F in an air fryer that has been preheated.

4. Make the potato quenelles as follows in the interim: Warm potatoes should be mashed. Mix in the nutmeg, milk, butter, salt, and pepper.

5. Transfer the potato mixture from one spoon to the other to form quenelles using two spoons. They can be prepared in advance and frozen until needed. You must cook them for about 10-15 minutes if you are using frozen ones. You must cook the quenelles for 8 minutes if they are freshly produced.

Brussels sprouts should be put in a bowl. Over it, drizzle some honey and olive oil. Well, toss.

7. Add the lamb to the air fryer along with the Brussels sprouts. Include the frozen quenelles as well.

8. Prepare for around 10-15 minutes. If using fresh quenelles, throw them in the air fryer 7 minutes after the Brussels sprouts are finished cooking.

Mojito Lamb Kabobs

Time needed for prep: 4 hours

Time needed to cook: 20 minutes

Serves: 2

Nutritional values per serving:

Ingredients:

- o 6 lamb loin chops, trimmed
- o Juice of 1half limes
- o 1 lime chopped into wedges
- o Zest of 1half limes, grated
- o 2 tbsps chopped fresh mint leaves
- o 1 tsp salt
- o quarter cup extra-virgin olive oil
- o 4 large cloves garlic, minced
- o quarter tsp pepper or to taste

Directions:

1. In a bowl, combine the lime zest, two limes' worth of juice, garlic, mint, salt, oil, and pepper.

2. Add the lamb and mix. Give the lamb a thorough coating of the mixture.

3. Cover, then leave out for four hours. Every hour, toss the meat.

4. Add lime wedges and a couple of air fryer skewers with the meat.

5. Depending on the level of doneness required, roast for 15-20 minutes in an air fryer that has been preheated to 370 °F.

Chapter 8 – Seafood Recipes

Air Fryer Salmon

Time needed for prep: 5 minutes

Time needed to cook: 8 minutes

Serves: 1

Nutritional values per serving:

Calories: 324

Fat: 14 g

Carb: 0 g

Fiber Content: 0 g

Total Protein: 45 g

Ingredients:

- half pd fresh Alaska king salmon
- Pepper as per taste
- quarter tsp chili powder
- Salt as per taste
- Chopped parsley to garnish
- 1 lime

Directions:

1. Season the salmon with salt, pepper, and chili powder.

2. Juice the remaining half of the lime after slicing it into thin slices.

3. Put the fish in the basket of the air fryer. Over the fish, scatter lime slices.

4. Fry in an air fryer that has been preheated to 375 °F for 8 minutes, or until the meatiest part's internal temperature registers 145 °F on a meat thermometer.

5. Top with lime juice and serve with parsley as a garnish.

Salmon Cakes

Time needed for prep: 25 minutes

Time needed to cook: 7–12 minutes

Serves: 2

Nutritional values per serving: (2 cakes):

Calories: 519

Fat: 29 g

Carb: 26.5 g

Fiber Content: 11 g

Total Protein: 41 g

Ingredients:

- o   half pd fresh Atlantic salmon
- o   2 tbsps cilantro (chopped), plus extra to garnish
- o   Salt as per taste
- o   1 brown egg, beaten
- o   Coconut oil to brush
- o   2 tbsps mashed avocado
- o   ¾ tsp yellow curry powder
- o   3 tbsps tapioca starch, divided
- o   quarter cup coconut flakes
- o   For greens:
- o   1 tsp melted coconut oil
- o   Salt as per taste
- o   3 cups tightly packed arugula and spinach mix

Directions:

1. Clean the salmon, removing any large bones and skin, and place it in a basin. Mix in the cilantro, avocado, salt, and curry powder thoroughly.

2. Stir in 1 tablespoon of tapioca starch.

3. Divide the mixture into 4 equal portions, then form each portion into patties. Put the patties on a tray that has been covered in parchment paper. Keep the tray in your freezer for 20 minutes or so.

4. Use coconut oil to grease the air fryer basket.

5. Add two tablespoons of tapioca starch to a small bowl. Add coconut flakes to a different small bowl.

6. Cooking spray the cakes on both sides before placing them in the air fryer basket.

7. Dredge the salmon cakes in the tapioca starch first. Dip next in the egg. Shake to remove any extra egg. Last but not least, coat only the top and sides with coconut flakes. To adhere, lightly press.

8. Put the side with the coconut flakes facing up in the air fryer basket with the salmon cakes.

9. Apply some melted coconut oil to the salmon cakes.

10. Cook until golden brown and crisp on the exterior and cooked and moist inside, about 15 minutes in an air fryer that has been preheated to 400 °F.

11. Because the cakes sometimes stick, you will need to remove them using a metal spatula.

12. Create the greens as follows in the interim: Set a pan on a moderate heat source. Heat after adding coconut oil. Saute the spinach, arugula, and salt until the spinach just begins to wilt. Turn off the heat.

13. Divide the greens between two plates. Serve with cilantro as a garnish and salmon cakes on top.

Healthy Baked Salmon

Time needed for prep: 2 minutes

Time needed to cook: 10 minutes

Serves: 1

Nutritional values per serving: (without broccoli):

Calories: 350

Fat: 23 g

Carb: 0 g

Fiber Content: 0 g

Total Protein: 35 g

Ingredients:

- o   1 salmon fillets (6 ounces)
- o   Salt as per taste

- o   Pepper as per taste
- o   1 tsp chili powder or to taste (optional)
- o   half tsp olive oil

Directions:

1. Oil the salmon fillets with a brush.

2. Add chili powder, salt, and pepper.

3. Bake for 10-15 minutes, or until desired doneness, in an air fryer that has been preheated to 360 °F. Halfway through baking, turn the fish.

4. If wanted, serve with roasted broccoli.

Fish Tacos

Time needed for prep: 30 minutes

Time needed to cook: 5 minutes

Serves: 3

Nutritional values per serving:

Calories: 250

Fat: 11 g

Carb: 26 g

Fiber Content: 3 g

Total Protein: 11 g

Ingredients:

- o   1 tbsp sour cream
- o   1 small clove garlic, chopped
- o   Salt as per taste
- o   1 onion (sliced)
- o   1 small egg
- o   quarter cup bread crumbs (panko)
- o   6 Old El Paso mini flour tortillas taco bowls
- o   quarter pd skinless white fish fillets, chop into one" strips

- o 2 tsps water
- o 1 tbsp taco seasoning mix
- o ¾ cup shredded green cabbage
- o half tsp lime juice
- o half tbsp mayonnaise
- o Cooking spray
- o For topping:
- o Avocado slices
- o Cilantro (chopped)
- o Radish slices
- o Lime wedges

Directions:

1. Fill a small bowl with taco seasoning.

2. In a another bowl, mix together the water and eggs.

3. Fill a third basin with salt and panko bread crumbs.

4. Fill the fourth bowl with mayonnaise, sour cream, garlic, salt, and lime juice. Stir thoroughly to mix.

5. Add the onion and cabbage. Before using, cover and chill.

6. Use parchment paper to line the air fryer basket.

7. To begin, sprinkle taco spice over the fish strips. Shake to release any extra seasoning. Dip next in the egg. Shake to remove any extra egg.

8. Lastly, coat with panko. Lightly press it to help the panko adhere to the fish.

9. After giving the fish a thorough cooking spraying, put it in the air fryer basket.

10. Cook in an air fryer that has been preheated to 350 °F for 12 to 16 minutes, or until well cooked. Halfway through frying, turn the fish.

11. Take the fish out and set it on a chopping board. Slice into pieces after it is cold enough to handle.

12. Fill the taco bowls with the cabbage mixture. Disperse fish.

13. Add the recommended toppings, then serve.

Shrimp Spring Rolls with Sweet Chili Sauce

Time needed for prep: 15 minutes

Time needed to cook: 15 minutes

Serves: 2

Nutritional values per serving: (2 spring rolls with 2 tbsps sauce):

Calories: 180

Fat: 9 g

Carb: 19 g

Fiber Content: 3 g

Total Protein: 7 g

Ingredients:

- o   3 tsps sesame oil, divided
- o   half cup matchstick carrot
- o   1 cup shredded cabbage
- o   half cup red peppers cut in julienne style
- o   ⅓ cup julienne-cut snow peas
- o   2 ounces peeled, deveined raw shrimp, chopped
- o   2 tbsps cilantro (chopped)
- o   1 tsp fish sauce
- o   8 spring roll wrappers (each of 8-inch square)
- o   half tbsp lime juice (freshly squeezed)
- o   Crushed red pepper as per taste
- o   quarter cup sweet chili sauce

Directions:

1. Set a skillet over a high heat. Add 1/4 teaspoon of oil. Add the carrot, cabbage, and bell pepper when the oil is almost smoking, and cook until the vegetables just start to wilt.

Transfer to a baking sheet in step two. Allow it to cool for a while.

3. Place the amalgamation in a basin. Along with the other ingredients, put the shrimp, cilantro, fish sauce, lime juice, snow peas, and crushed red pepper in the bowl.

4. Arrange the spring roll wrappers so that one of the corners is facing you on your countertop.

5. Place one-fourth cup of filling in the center (3 inches long, along the line from the other 2 diagonally opposite corners).

6. Cover the filling with the corner that is facing you. Additionally, fold the right and left corners over the filling (like folding an envelope). Roll firmly in the direction of the final corner.

7. Spray a little water into the final corner. To ensure adhesion, press the final corner.

8. Spread the spring rolls with the remaining oil.

9. Liberally spritz the air fryer basket with cooking spray. Put spring rolls in the basket of the air fryer.

10. Depending on how crisp you like it, air fried at 390 °F for 8 minutes or until the outside is a light golden brown. Spring rolls should be turned after 4 minutes of frying.

11. Offer as a dip with sweet chili sauce.

Air Fryer Lemon Pepper Shrimp

Time needed for prep: 5 minutes

Time needed to cook: 6-8 minutes per batch

Serves: 4

Nutritional values per serving:

Calories: 215

Fat: 8.6 g

Carb: 12.6 g

Fiber Content: 5.5 g

Total Protein: 28.59 g

Ingredients:

- o 2 tbsps olive oil
- o 2 tsps lemon pepper
- o half tsp garlic powder
- o 2 lemons, sliced, to serve
- o Juice of 2 lemons
- o half tsp paprika
- o 24 ounces raw medium shrimp, peeled, deveined

Directions:

1. In a large bowl, combine all of the ingredients (except the shrimp) and stir well.

2. Add the shrimp and well-toss.

3. Use batch cooking.

4. Cook for 6 to 8 minutes at 400 °F in an air fryer that has been preheated, or until they are firm to the touch and pink in color.

5. Add lemon slices and serve hot.

Shrimp Fried Rice

Time needed for prep: 50-60 minutes

Time needed to cook: 10 minutes

Serves: 4

Nutritional values per serving:

Calories: 410

Fat: 6.5 g

Carb: 54 g

Fiber Content: 0 g

Total Protein: 32 g

Ingredients:

- o 2 cups instant rice
- o 12 ounces cooked shrimp
- o 12.7 ounces stir-fry vegetables
- o 4 tbsps sweet and tangy sauce
- o 4 large eggs, whisked
- o 4 tsps soy sauce

Directions:

1. Prepare the instant rice as directed on the packet.

2. Allow to fully cool. Place in a basin. Mix in the stir-fried veggie mixture and soy sauce. If necessary, cook in batches.

3. Fill the air fryer baking accessory with rice.

4. Air fried for 10 minutes at 400 °F in a preheated air fryer. Incorporate into a bowl.

5. Stir in the sauce, shrimp, and eggs.

6. Prepare for eight minutes. While cooking, stir a couple of times.

Air Fryer Scallops

Time needed for prep: 10 minutes

Time needed to cook: 6 minutes

Serves: 1

Nutritional values per serving:

Calories: 348

Fat: 30 g

Carb: 5 g

Fiber Content: 0 g

Total Protein: 14 g

Ingredients:

- o   4 large sea scallops, cleaned, pat dried
- o   Salt as per taste
- o   2 tbsps extra-virgin olive oil
- o   1 tsp capers, very chopped
- o   1 small clove garlic, minced
- o   Pepper as per taste
- o   1 tbsp minced parsley
- o   half tsp finely lemon zest (grated)
- o   Cooking spray

Directions:

1. Spray cooking spray in the basket of the air fryer. Place the scallops in the air fryer basket after seasoning with salt and pepper.

2. Fry for 6 minutes at 400 °F in an air fryer that has been preheated, or until the internal temperature reaches 120 °F.

Remove 3. Place on a dish.

4. Combine the ingredients in a bowl and whisk to combine. Serve the scallops with a spoon.

Southern Style Catfish with Green Beans

Time needed for prep: 10 minutes

Time needed to cook: 20 minutes

Serves: 1

Nutritional values per serving:

Calories: 416

Fat: 18 g

Carb: 31 g

Fiber Content: 7 g

Total Protein: 33 g

Ingredients:

- o 6 ounces fresh green beans, trimmed
- o half tsp light brown sugar
- o Salt as per taste
- o 2 tbsps flour (all purpose)
- o 3 tbsps bread crumbs (panko)
- o 1 tbsp mayonnaise
- o half tsp dill pickle relish
- o A pinch granulated sugar
- o quarter tsp crushed red pepper (optional)
- o 1 catfish fillet
- o 1 small egg, lightly beaten
- o Pepper as per taste

- o 1 tsp minced fresh dill
- o quarter tsp apple cider vinegar
- o Lemon wedges to serve

Directions:

Green beans should be put into a bowl. Give the beans a good coating of cooking spray and stir thoroughly.

2. Sprinkle salt, brown sugar, and red pepper flakes over the beans. Well, toss.

3. Insert into the basket of an air fryer.

4. Roast for 12 minutes, or until browned and tender, in an air fryer that has been preheated to 400 °F.

5. Place the beans in a serving bowl. Put the bowl aside and cover it with foil.

On a dish, scatter the flour. Put panko (bread crumbs) on a different plate.

7. Flour-dredge the catfish first. Shake to remove any extra flour. Dip next in the egg. Shake to remove any extra egg. Finally, coat in panko bread crumbs and put in air fryer basket.

8. Apply some frying spray to the fillet.

9. Roast for 8 minutes at 400 °F in an air fryer that has been preheated, or until well cooked inside and crisp on the exterior.

10. Remove from air fryer and salt before serving.

11. Prepare the sauce as follows in the interim: In a bowl, combine the mayonnaise, vinegar, sugar, dill, and dill pickle relish. Whisk to combine.

12. Arrange roasted catfish fillet on a plate with roasted green beans, sauce, and lemon wedges.

Roasted Salmon with Fennel Salad

Time needed for prep: 15 minutes

Time needed to cook: 8–10 minutes

Serves: 2

Nutritional values per serving:

Calories: 464

Fat: 30 g

Carb: 9 g

Fiber Content: 3 g

Total Protein: 38 g

Ingredients:

- o 1 tsp chopped fresh parsley
- o half tsp kosher salt, divided
- o 1 tbsp olive oil
- o ⅓ cup low-fat 2% Yogurt (Greek)
- o 1 tbsp fresh orange juice
- o 1 tbsp chopped fresh dill
- o half tsp minced fresh thyme
- o 2 salmon fillets (6 ounces each), skinless, center-cut
- o 2 cups thinly sliced fennel
- o 1 small clove garlic, peeled, grated
- o half tsp fresh lime juice

Directions:

1. Combine salt, thyme, parsley, and dill in a basin.

2. Oil the fish with a brush. Place the salmon in the air fryer basket and evenly distribute the herb mixture over it.

3. Roast for 8 to 10 minutes, depending on desired doneness, in an air fryer that has been preheated to 350 °F.

4. Construct the fennel salad in the interim as follows: In a bowl, combine all the remaining ingredients and stir thoroughly.

5. Split the fennel salad between two dishes. Serve the dish with salmon fillets on top.

Fish en Papillote

Time needed for prep: 10 minutes

Time needed to cook: 15 minutes

Serves: 4

Nutritional values per serving:

Calories: 251

Fat: 12 g

Carb: 8 g

Fiber Content: 2 g

Total Protein: 26 g

Ingredients:

- 3-4 tbsps butter, melted
- Ground pepper as per taste
- Salt as per taste
- 4 cod fillets (5 ounces each), thawed
- 1 cup sliced bulb fennel
- 1 cup sliced carrot
- 1 cup red peppers (sliced)
- 4 sprigs tarragon or 1 tsp dried tarragon
- 2 tbsps lime juice
- 2 tbsps oil

Directions:

1. In a bowl, combine the butter, tarragon, salt, and lime juice. veggies, then stir in.

2. On your tabletop, spread out 4 sizable squares of parchment paper.

3. Use oil to mist the fillets. Each sheet of parchment paper should have a fillet on it. Season with salt and pepper. Vegetables should be divided and arranged over the fillets.

4. To create packets, fold the parchment paper over the fillets. To ensure that the fillets stay in the packets, press the edges firmly.

5. Use the air fryer to cook the packets. Make batches of food.

6. Air fry for roughly 15 minutes at 350 °F in a preheated air fryer. Take it out of the air fryer and give it three to four minutes to rest.

7. Immediately before serving, open the packets.

Fish and Chips

Time needed for prep: 15 minutes

Time needed to cook: 20 minutes

Serves: 2

Nutritional values per serving:

Calories: 415

Fat: 7 g

Carb: 46 g

Fiber Content: 4 g

Total Protein: 44 g

Ingredients:

- o   1 large russet potato, scrubbed
- o   Salt as per taste
- o   1 egg
- o   half cup bread crumbs (panko)
- o   quarter cup malt vinegar
- o   half cup flour (all purpose)
- o   1 tbsp water
- o   2 tilapia fillets (6 ounces each), skinless, halved lengthwise

Directions:

1. Use a spiralizer to create spirals out of the potatoes.

2. Use batch cooking. In the air fryer basket, distribute spiralized potatoes. Cooking spray should be applied to it. Toss thoroughly and re-spray until thoroughly coated.

3. Air-fry for 10 minutes at 390 °F in an air fryer that has been preheated. When the potatoes are halfway done, turn them.

Take the food out of the air fryer. Set aside after adding salt.

5. In the meantime, combine some flour and salt in a small basin.

6. In a another bowl, mix together the water and eggs.

7. Fill a third basin with salt and panko bread crumbs.

8. Roll the fish strips in the flour mixture to start. Shake to remove any extra flour. Dip next in the egg. Shake to remove any extra egg.

9. Lastly, coat with panko. Lightly press it to help the panko adhere to the fish.

10. After giving the fish a thorough coating of cooking spray, put it in the air fryer basket.

11. Cook for 10 minutes at 375 °F in an air fryer that has been preheated. Halfway through frying, turn the fish.

12. Place two fish slices on each plate. Place the potato spirals on each plate, then add 2 tbsp. of malt vinegar for dipping.

Chapter 9 - Seafood Recipes

Coconut Shrimp

Time needed for prep: 10 minutes

Time needed to cook: 15 minutes

Serves: 2

Nutritional values per serving:

Calories: 250

Fat: 9 g

Carb: 30 g

Fiber Content: 2 g

Total Protein: 15 g

Ingredients:

- o   quarter cup flour (all purpose)
- o   12 medium shrimp, peeled, deveined
- o   1 egg
- o   ⅓ cup shredded unsweetened coconut
- o   ⅛ tsp cayenne pepper (optional)
- o   ¾ tsp pepper
- o   quarter cup bread crumbs (panko)
- o   quarter tsp salt
- o   Cooking spray
- o   For the dip:
- o   2 tbsps lime juice
- o   2 tbsps honey
- o   half Serrano chili, thinly sliced

Directions:

1. In a small bowl, combine the flour, salt, and pepper.

2. Put bread crumbs in a bowl that is not too deep. Bread crumbs in a bowl; add salt, cayenne pepper, and coconut; stir thoroughly.

3. In a different bowl, whisk the egg.

4. Dust flour on the shrimp.

5. Dip in the egg next. Shake any extra egg off. Enter the combination of bread crumbs. Place on a baking sheet after giving a gentle press. Use cooking spray to spritz.

6. Put the shrimp in the basket of the air fryer.

7. Fry for 6 to 8 minutes in an air fryer that has been preheated to 400 °F. Halfway through baking, turn the shrimp.

8. Place all of the dip's ingredients in a bowl and whisk to combine.

9. Provide dip and coconut shrimp.

Hot and Sweet Coconut Shrimp and Apricot Sauce

Time needed for prep: 25 minutes

Time needed to cook: 10 minutes

Serves: 3

Nutritional values per serving:

Calories: 410

Fat: 10 g

Carb: 58 g

Fiber Content: 2 g

Total Protein: 24 g

Ingredients:

- o ¾ pd raw large shrimp, peeled, deveined, with tail on
- o quarter cup bread crumbs (panko)
- o 12 tsps Louisiana-style hot sauce
- o Pepper as per taste
- o Salt as per taste

- ¾ cup sweetened, shredded coconut
- 2 large egg whites
- quarter cup flour (all purpose)
- For the sauce:
- half cup apricot preserves
- ⅛ tsp crushed red pepper flakes
- half tsp apple cider vinegar

Directions:

1. Combine bread crumbs and coconut in a small basin and whisk.

2. Add and thoroughly whisk the egg whites in another small basin.

3. Fill a third small basin with flour.

4. Dredge the shrimp in flour first. Shake to release additional flour.

5. After that, dip in the egg. Shake to remove any extra egg. Dredge in the bread crumbs mixture lastly. To adhere, lightly press. If necessary, cook in batches.

6. Liberally spritz the air fryer basket with cooking spray. Put shrimp in the basket of the air fryer.

7. Air fry at 375 °F for 8 minutes, or until the inside is pink and the outside is light brown. After 4 minutes of frying, flip the sides.

8. Fill a saucepan with the sauce's necessary ingredients. Set the pan to medium heat. Till the mixture melts, stir constantly.

9. If preferred, top rice with spicy shrimp and apricot sauce.

Crab Cakes

Time needed for prep: 10 minutes

Time needed to cook: 10 minutes

Serves: 2

Nutritional values per serving:

Calories: 185

Fat: 13.2 g

Carb: 2.4 g

Fiber Content: 1.1 g

Total Protein: 13.5 g

Ingredients:

For the crab cakes:

- o 4 ounces lump crabmeat
- o 1 small egg, beaten
- o 1 tbsp chopped fresh parsley
- o quarter tsp Old Bay seasoning or any other fish seasoning
- o Pepper as per taste
- o Salt as per taste
- o half tbsp mayonnaise
- o 1 tbsp melted butter
- o 2 tbsps almond flour
- o 2 tbsps green onion (sliced fine)
- o 1 tsp Dijon mustard
- o For spicy mayonnaise:
- o A dash of sriracha sauce or any other hot sauce
- o 2 tbsps mayonnaise
- o Cajun seasoning to taste

Directions:

1. Fill a bowl with crab meat. Bread the meat with a fork.

2. Stir in the almond flour, Old Bay seasoning, parsley, green onion, pepper, and salt until thoroughly combined.

3. Add the egg mustard and mayonnaise, and combine thoroughly.

4. Divide the mixture into two equal amounts and form patties that are about an inch thick.

5. Use waxed paper to cover a platter. The crab cakes should be placed on a platter and chilled for 30 to 60 minutes.

6. Use cooking spray to grease the air fryer rack. Insert the rack into the air fryer.

7. Place the crab cakes on the rack and brush with melted butter.

8. Air-fry for 8 minutes at 375 °F in a preheated air fryer, or until pink within and light brown outside. After 4 minutes of frying, flip the sides.

9. To create the dip, combine mayonnaise, Cajun seasoning, and Sriracha sauce in a bowl.

10. Offer the crab cakes alongside the dip.

Shrimp Scampi

Time needed for prep: 5 minutes

Time needed to cook: 10 minutes

Serves: 2

Nutritional values per serving:

Calories: 221

Fat: 13 g

Carb: 1 g

Fiber Content: 0 g

Total Protein: 23 g

Ingredients:

- 2 tbsps butter
- half tbsp garlic, minced
- half tbsp chives (chopped) or half tsp dried chives
- 1 tbsp chicken stock or white wine
- half tbsp lime juice
- 1 tsp red pepper flakes
- half tbsp fresh basil leaves (minced) or half tsp dried basil, plus extra for garnishing
- half pd shrimp (about 10–12), thawed

Directions:

1. Set the air fryer's accessory baking pan inside and let it to heat to 330 °F.

2. Heat up the butter, garlic, and red pepper flakes in the pan. For a few minutes, cook. only time.

3. Combine the ingredients and whisk them.

4. Prepare for five minutes. The pan should be taken out of the air fryer and left to rest for a moment.

5. Stir and serve with basil as a garnish.

Chapter 10 - Meatless and Vegan Recipes

French Fry Po' Boy (Cajun)

Time needed for prep: 10 minutes

Time needed to cook: 30 minutes

Serves: 2

Nutritional values per serving:

Calories: 249

Fat: 6 g

Carb: 43 g

Fiber Content: 3 g

Total Protein: 7 g

Ingredients:

For the French fries:

- o 2 medium Idaho russet potatoes, chop into fries
- o 1 tsp olive oil
- o quarter tsp smoked paprika
- o ⅛ tsp garlic powder
- o 3 cups boiling water
- o half tsp Cajun seasoning blend
- o quarter tsp salt
- o Pepper as per taste

For the mushroom gravy:

- o half tbsp olive oil
- o 1 tsp soy sauce
- o quarter cup water
- o half tbsp tapioca starch
- o 1half cups chopped mushrooms
- o 1 tsp vegan Worcestershire sauce
- o For the sandwich:
- o 2 fresh soft French loaf or Italian bread
- o Lettuce leaves
- o Tomato slices
- o Hot sauce

- o   Vegan mayonnaise

Directions:

1. Put the potatoes in a container. Sprinkle it with boiling water. Allow it to soak for 10 to 15 minutes. The potatoes should be drained and dried with a kitchen towel.

2. Arrange the fries in a bowl and top with oil. Well, toss. Toss thoroughly after adding salt, pepper, paprika, garlic, and Cajun flavor.

3. Spray the air fryer basket with cooking spray liberally.

4. Insert into the basket of an air fryer. Distribute it evenly.

5. Air fried for 10 minutes at 350 °F in a preheated air fryer. Halfway through the frying process, shake the basket.

6. Raise the temperature to 390 °F and cook the food for an additional 10 minutes, stirring the basket halfway through.

7. When the heat is moderate, put a skillet on the stove. Add one-half tbsp of olive oil. Add the mushrooms to the hot oil and sauté them until the cooked juices come to the surface.

8. Stir in the Worcestershire sauce and soy sauce. For a few minutes, cook.

9. In a bowl, combine water and tapioca starch; pour the mixture into the skillet.

10. Increase the heat to medium-high and stir continuously until the mixture thickens.

11. Horizontally split the loaf in half. If preferred, toast the bread.

12. Drizzle it with vegan mayonnaise. Spread lettuce and tomato slices over the bread's bottom half.

13. Evenly distribute the fries and arrange them on top of the tomato pieces. Add a mushroom on top. Serve with the loaf's top half on top.

Sticky Mushroom Rice

Time needed for prep: 5 minutes

Time needed to cook: 20 minutes

Serves: 3

Nutritional values per serving: (1 cup):

Calories: 366

Fat: 0 g

Carb: 77 g

Fiber Content: 2 g

Total Protein: 10 g

Ingredients:

- o 8 ounces jasmine rice, uncooked
- o 2 tbsps maple syrup
- o 1 tsp Chinese 5 spice powder
- o 2 tbsps white wine or rice vinegar
- o quarter cup frozen peas
- o quarter cup soy sauce or tamari
- o 2 cloves garlic, chopped
- o quarter tsp ground ginger
- o 8 ounces cremini mushrooms, in halves or in quarters, depending on the size

Directions:

1. Prepare rice using the directions on the package.

2. In the meantime, combine the following ingredients in a bowl: maple syrup, tamari, white wine, five-spice powder, garlic, and ground ginger.

3. Add the mushrooms to the baking accessory for the air fryer.

4. Air fried for 10 minutes at 350 °F in a preheated air fryer.

5. Give the mushrooms a stir. Over the mushrooms, pour the sauce mixture. Add some peas on top. Well combine, then cook for 5 minutes.

6. Add the transfer to the rice pot and thoroughly stir.

7. Present hot.

Herb and Cheese Frittata

Time needed for prep: 10 minutes

Time needed to cook: 12–15 minutes

Serves: 2

Nutritional values per serving:

Calories: 141

Fat: 10 g

Carb: 2 g

Fiber Content: 0 g

Total Protein: 8 g

Ingredients:

- o   2 eggs
- o   3 tbsps cheddar cheese (grated)
- o   1 tbsp cilantro (chopped) or parsley
- o   quarter tsp pepper
- o   quarter tsp salt
- o   quarter cup half-and-half
- o   1 tbsp chopped green scallions

Directions:

1. Liberally spray cooking spray on the air fryer baking accessory.

2. Whisk together the eggs and half-and-half in a bowl.

3. Combine all of the ingredients by stirring in the cheddar cheese, cilantro, salt, and pepper.

4. Pour into the baking dish that has been prepared and set it in the air fryer basket.

5. Bake for 12 to 15 minutes, or until set, in a preheated air fryer at 330 °F.

6. If preferred, let cool for a few minutes. Serve after cutting into wedges.

Grilled American Cheese Sandwich

Time needed for prep: 2 minutes

Time needed to cook: 8 minutes per sandwich

Serves: 2

Nutritional values per serving:

Calories: 429

Fat: 28 g

Carb: 25 g

Fiber Content: 1 g

Total Protein: 18 g

Ingredients:

- o 4 slices sandwich bread
- o 4 tsps butter
- o 4 slices cheddar cheese

Directions:

On a dish, arrange two slices of bread. Put a cheese slice on each.

2. Add the final 2 slices of bread to form a covering.

3. Cover the outside of each sandwich with butter. If necessary, cook in batches.

4. Grill for 4 minutes at 330 °F in an air fryer that has been preheated. Cook the opposite side for 4 minutes after flipping the sides.

Crispy Toasted Sesame Tofu

Time needed for prep: 15 minutes

Time needed to cook: 45 minutes

Serves: 2

Nutritional values per serving:

Calories: 445

Fat: 20 g

Carb: 46 g

Fiber Content: 3 g

Total Protein: 23 g

Ingredients:

- o 1 package tofu (extra-firm), drained, chop into one" cubes
- o 2 tbsps fresh orange juice
- o 2 tsps honey
- o half tsp rice vinegar
- o 1 package boil-in-bag brown rice
- o 1 tbsp chopped scallions
- o 1 tbsp soy sauce (low-sodium)
- o half tbsp plus half tsp toasted sesame oil
- o quarter tsp cornflour
- o Kosher salt as per taste
- o half tbsp toasted sesame seeds
- o Cooking spray

Directions:

1. Press any extra moisture from the tofu. Tofu can be done by layering paper towels on top of it. Additionally, spread some paper towels over the tofu. Over the tofu, place something substantial, such as a large pan. Allow it to drain for thirty minutes.

2. Use cooking spray to coat the tofu. Transfer to the basket of an air fryer. It should be spread out in one layer.

3. Air-fry for about 10-15 minutes, or until golden brown, in an air fryer that has been preheated to 375 °F. While cooking, shake the basket a couple of times. Incorporate into a bowl.

4. Prepare the rice in the meantime using the directions on the package. Rice is added; stir. Place aside.

5. Combine rice vinegar, cornflour, honey, orange juice, sesame oil, and soy sauce in a small saucepan. Stir thoroughly.

6. Heat the saucepan to a high temperature. Up until the sauce thickens, stir continuously.

Pour on top of the tofu. Mix thoroughly until coated.

8. To put it all together, divide the rice between two bowls. Place the tofu over the rice after being divided.

9. Add scallions and sesame seeds as a garnish before serving.

Twice-Fried Vegan Stuffed Potatoes

Time needed for prep: 15 minutes

Time needed to cook: 35 minutes

Serves: 2

Nutritional values per serving:

Calories: 121

Fat: 2 g

Carb: 22 g

Fiber Content: 2 g

Total Protein: 5 g

Ingredients:

- o 1 large Idaho russet baking potato
- o 2 tbsps unsweetened vegan yogurt
- o 1 tbsp nutritional yeast
- o Pepper as per taste
- o 1 tsp olive oil
- o 2 tbsps nondairy milk
- o quarter tsp salt substitute
- o half cup chopped spinach or kale
- o Optional toppings:
- o 2 tbsps vegan yogurt
- o 1 tsp chopped herbs of your choice
- o Smoked salt
- o Pepper

Directions:

1. Oil the potato thoroughly. Rub it in thoroughly.

2. Put the potato in the basket of the air fryer.

3. Air-fry for about 60 minutes, or until fork tender, at 390 °F in a preheated air fryer.

4. Halfway through baking, turn the potato.

5. Take the potato out of the oven and give it some time to cool. Cut the potato in half lengthwise when it is safe to handle.

6. Remove the potato cases from the potato halves and scoop out the centers.

7. Scoop out the potato and mash it in a bowl. Mix well before adding vegan yogurt, nondairy milk, pepper, salt, and nutritional yeast.

8. Stir in the spinach.

9. Fill the potato cases with this mixture.

10. Put the potato cases that have been filled in the air fryer.

11. Bake for 5-7 minutes at 350 °F.

12. If using, top with the recommended toppings and serve.

Easy Seitan Riblets

Time needed for prep: 15 minutes

Time needed to cook: 20 minutes

Serves: 2

Nutritional values per serving:

Calories: 272

Fat: 2 g

Carb: 19 g

Fiber Content: 3 g

Total Protein: 47 g

Ingredients:

- o half cup vital wheat gluten
- o half tsp mushroom powder
- o half tsp salt (optional)
- o 6 tbsps water
- o 2 tbsps nutritional yeast
- o half tsp onion powder
- o quarter tsp garlic powder
- o 2 tbsps BBQ sauce

Directions:

1. Fill the food processor bowl with all the ingredients listed, excluding the water (fix the dough attachment). Blend thoroughly after processing.

2. Run a tiny stream of water through the feeder tube (with the food processor running).

3. Continue processing until dough forms.

4. Remove the dough and set it on the counter. Use your hands to knead the dough for a couple more minutes.

5. Roll out the dough, divide it into two pieces, and place them in the air fryer.

6. Air fried for 8 minutes at 370 °F in a preheated air fryer. Cook for another 4-5 minutes after flipping the sides.

7. Snip the food out of the air fryer and chop it into the appropriate shape. Place in the baking attachment for an air fryer.

8. Top with barbecue sauce.

9. Cook the pan for 5 minutes in the air fryer.

Crispy Vegetable Quesadilla

Time needed for prep: 15 minutes

Time needed to cook: 20 minutes

Serves: 2

Nutritional values per serving:

Calories: 291

Fat: 8 g

Carb: 36 g

Fiber Content: 8 g

Total Protein: 17 g

Ingredients:

- 2 sprouted whole-grain flour tortillas (6 inches each)
- half cup sliced red peppers
- half cup unsalted canned or cooked black beans, drained, rinsed
- 1 ounce plain 2% reduced-fat Yogurt (Greek)

- o   ⅛ tsp cumin powder
- o   quarter cup drained, refrigerated pico de gallo
- o   half cup grated cheddar cheese
- o   half cup sliced zucchini
- o   half tsp grated lime zest
- o   half tbsp lime juice (freshly squeezed)
- o   1 tbsp chopped, fresh cilantro

Directions:

1. Arrange your countertop with the tortillas. Place around 2 tbsp of cheese on each tortilla half. Spread the cheese with the zucchini, red pepper, and black beans. Top with the remaining cheese.

2. Fold the second tortilla half over the filling. Spray some cooking spray on the outside. With toothpicks, secure.

3. Insert the air fryer basket with the quesadillas inside.

4. Air-fry for 10 minutes or until crisp in an air fryer that has been preheated to 400 °F. Halfway through frying, flip the sides.

5. To make cumin cream, combine yogurt, lime juice, zest, and cumin in a bowl and stir to combine.

6. Take the quesadillas out of the air fryer and cut each one into wedges. Serve with cumin cream, pico de gallo, and cilantro as garnish.

Vegetarian Tacos

Time needed for prep: 5 minutes

Time needed to cook: 20 minutes

Serves: 2

Nutritional values per serving:

Calories: 251

Fat: 8 g

Carb: 35 g

Fiber Content: 8 g

Total Protein: 11 g

Ingredients:

- half can (from a 15-ounce can) cooked kidney beans, drained, rinsed
- 1 clove garlic, peeled, thinly sliced
- quarter tsp chili powder or to taste
- 1.8 ounces crumbled feta cheese (optional)
- 1 tbsp cilantro (chopped)
- 2 taco shells or tortillas
- 1 onion, thinly sliced
- half can (from a 15-ounce can) tomatoes (crushed or chopped)
- half tsp cumin powder
- quarter tsp coriander powder
- quarter red onion, thinly sliced
- 1 lime, quartered
- Salt as per taste
- Pepper as per taste

Directions:

1. Fill the baking accessory for the air fryer with the kidney beans, onion, tomato, garlic, salt, and pepper.

2. Air-fry for 10 to 15 minutes at 350 °F in a preheated air fryer. While cooking, stir a couple of times.

3. Arrange the tortillas on the tabletop. Among the tortillas, distribute the bean mixture.

4. Top with feta, cilantro, and red onion before serving.

Chapter 11 - Side Dish Recipes

Loaded Potatoes

Time needed for prep: 10 minutes

Time needed to cook: 15 minutes

Serves: 1

Nutritional values per serving: (4 small potatoes):

Calories: 199

Fat: 7 g

Carb: 26 g

Fiber Content: 4 g

Total Protein: 7 g

Ingredients:

- o 5 ounces baby Yukon gold potatoes (4 potatoes of about 2 inches each)
- o 1 center-cut bacon slice
- o 1 tbsp shredded low-fat cheddar cheese
- o Salt as per taste
- o half tsp olive oil
- o 2 tsps chives (chopped)
- o 1 tbsp low-fat sour cream

Directions:

1. Start a pan on a moderate heat.

2. Add the slice of bacon to the pan.

3. Heat until golden.

4. Using a spoon, remove the bacon and place it on a plate covered in paper towels. Don't throw away the pan's fat. When the bacon is safe to handle, crumble it.

5. In the meantime, put the potatoes in a container and cover it with oil. Well, toss.

6. Insert into the basket of an air fryer. Distribute it evenly.

7. Air-fry at 350 °F for 25 minutes, or until fork tender, in a preheated air fryer. While cooking, shake the basket a few times.

8. Take the potatoes out of the oven. When the potatoes are cool enough to handle, lightly crush each one until it splits in half.

9. Spread the split potatoes with the leftover fat in the pan.

10. Add cheese, bacon, chives, salt, and pepper.

11. Top with sour cream and serve.

Baked Garlic Parsley Potatoes

Time needed for prep: 5 minutes

Time needed to cook: 35 minutes

Serves: 6

Nutritional values per serving:

Calories: 213

Fat: 4 g

Carb: 30 g

Fiber Content: 2 g

Total Protein: 4 g

Ingredients:

- o   3-4 tbsps olive oil
- o   6 Idaho or russet potatoes, scrubbed, rinsed
- o   Coarse sea salt as per taste
- o   2 tsps minced parsley, plus extra to garnish
- o   2 tbsps finely crushed garlic

Directions:

1. Place aluminum foil inside the air fryer basket.

2. Use a fork to poke holes all over the potatoes.

3. Drizzle the potatoes with oil, parsley, garlic, and sea salt. Put it in the air fryer basket after giving it a thorough rubdown.

4. Bake for 30-45 minutes, or until fork tender, in an air fryer that has been preheated to 350 °F. During baking, the potatoes should be turned a few times.

5. Garnish with parsley and serve hot, seasoned with salt and pepper.

Cauliflower Stir-Fry

Time needed for prep: 5 minutes

Time needed to cook: 25 minutes

Serves: 2

Nutritional values per serving:

Calories: 93

Fat: 3 g

Carb: 12 g

Fiber Content: 3 g

Total Protein: 4 g

Ingredients:

- o 1 small head cauliflower, chop into florets
- o 3 cloves garlic, finely sliced
- o half tbsp rice vinegar
- o half tbsp sriracha or hot sauce of your choice or add more if you like it spicy
- o 1 chopped onion, thinly sliced
- o ¾ tbsp tamari
- o quarter tsp coconut sugar or sugar
- o 1 scallion, sliced, to garnish

Directions:

1. Put the cauliflower in the air fryer's baking attachment.

2. Air-fry for 10 minutes at 350 °F in a preheated air fryer. After five minutes, shake the basket.

3. Stir in the onion. another 10 minutes of cooking.

4. Add the garlic and stir. five more minutes of cooking.

5. In a bowl, combine the soy sauce, coconut sugar, salt, vinegar, sriracha, and pepper. Whisk to combine.

6. Pour on top of the kamut. Well, toss.

5. Continue to cook.

8. Add scallions as a garnish and serve.

Crispy Onion Rings

Time needed for prep: 15 minutes

Time needed to cook: 10 minutes

Serves: 2

Nutritional values per serving: (6-7 onion rings with 2 tbsps sauce):

Calories: 174

Fat: 5 g

Carb: 25 g

Fiber Content: 3 g

Total Protein: 7 g

Ingredients:

- o quarter cup flour (all purpose)
- o Kosher salt as per taste
- o half tbsp water
- o 5 ounces sweet onion, chop into half-inch-thick rounds
- o 1 small egg
- o half cup bread crumbs (panko)
- o half tsp smoked paprika
- o Cooking spray
- o For the sauce:
- o 2 tbsps 1% low-fat Yogurt (Greek)
- o half tbsp ketchup
- o ⅛ tsp garlic powder
- o 1 tbsp canola mayonnaise
- o half tsp Dijon mustard
- o A large pinch paprika

Directions:

1. In a bowl, combine the flour, salt, and smoked paprika.

2. Add some salt and bread crumbs (panko) to another bowl.

3. In a third bowl, thoroughly mix the egg and water.

4. Distinguish the onion rings (from the slices).

5. To begin, coat onion slices with the flour mixture. Then, cover it with egg mixture. Shake to remove any extra egg, then roll it in the bread crumbs. Put the onion rings in the basket of the air fryer. Spray the onion rings with cooking spray liberally.

6. Air-fry at 360 °F for 7-8 minutes, or until golden brown, in a preheated air fryer. Halfway through frying, flip the sides. After turning the sides, spray some oil.

7. In the meantime, combine all of the sauce's ingredients in a bowl by adding them and stirring.

8. Split into 2 plates and top with sauce.

Baked Sweet Potato

Time needed for prep: 5 minutes

Time needed to cook: 35 minutes

Serves: 6

Nutritional values per serving: (without topping):

Calories: 153

Fat: 4 g

Carb: 26 g

Fiber Content: 3 g

Total Protein: 2 g

Ingredients:

- o   3-4 tbsps olive oil
- o   6 sweet potatoes, scrubbed, rinsed
- o   Coarse sea salt as per taste

Directions:

1. Place aluminum foil inside the air fryer basket.

2. Use a fork to make holes all over the sweet potatoes.

3. Season the sweet potatoes with sea salt and olive oil. Put it in the air fryer basket after giving it a thorough rubdown.

4. Bake for 35 minutes at 350 °F in an air fryer that has been preheated. During baking, the potatoes should be turned a few times.

5. Serve hot, seasoned with salt & pepper and your preferred additional toppings.

Herbed Brussels Sprouts

Time needed for prep: 10 minutes

Time needed to cook: 10 minutes

Serves: 2

Nutritional values per serving:

Calories: 79

Fat: 2 g

Carb: 12 g

Fiber Content: 4 g

Total Protein: 4 g

Ingredients:

- half pd Brussels sprouts, trimmed
- half tsp dried parsley
- quarter tsp dried thyme
- half tbsp olive oil
- half tsp garlic powder
- Salt as per taste

Directions:

1. Combine all of the ingredients in a bowl and stir thoroughly.

2. Put in the basket of the air fryer.

3. Roasting for 8 to 10 minutes, or until browned and crisp, in an air fryer that has been preheated to 390 °F. About halfway through cooking, shake the basket.

Cilantro Ranch Sweet Potato Cauliflower Patties

Time needed for prep: 15 minutes

Time needed to cook: 18–20 minutes

Serves: 4

Nutritional values per serving: (1):

Calories: 85

Fat: 2.9 g

Carb: 9 g

Fiber Content: 3.5 g

Total Protein: 2.7 g

Ingredients:

- o   1 medium sweet potato, peeled, chopped into chunks
- o   2 tbsps chopped green onion
- o   1 tbsp ranch seasoning
- o   quarter tsp chili powder
- o   1 tbsp arrowroot starch
- o   2 tbsp sunflower seeds or pumpkin seeds
- o   Pepper as per taste
- o   Salt as per taste
- o   1 cup cauliflower florets
- o   half tsp crushed garlic
- o   half cup packed cilantro (chopped)
- o   A pinch cumin
- o   2 tbsps ground flaxseeds
- o   Dipping sauce of your choice

Directions:

1. Fill the food processor bowl with the sweet potato. till the size is less, process.

2. Process the cauliflower, onion, and garlic until the cauliflower is broken up into smaller bits.

3. Once everything is combined and dough-like, add the sunflower seeds, arrowroot, flaxseed, cilantro, cumin, ranch seasoning, chili powder, salt, and pepper.

4. Divide the mixture into 4 equal amounts and form patties.

5. Put in the basket of the air fryer.

6. Air fried for 18 to 20 minutes at 370 °F in a preheated air fryer. Halfway through cooking, flip the sides.

Garlic Bread

Time needed for prep: 5 minutes

Time needed to cook: 5 minutes

Serves: 2

Nutritional values per serving: (2 slices):

Calories: 290

Fat: 12 g

Carb: 35 g

Fiber Content: 3 g

Total Protein: 10 g

Ingredients:

- o   4 slices ciabatta
- o   2 cloves garlic, finely minced
- o   2 tbsps freshly parmesan cheese (grated)
- o   half tbsp salted butter
- o   A pinch dried parsley

Directions:

1. Put butter in a small microwave-safe bowl. To soften, raise the microwave's temperature for 8 to 10 seconds.

2. Include cheese, parsley, and garlic.

3. Apply the garlic butter mixture on slices of ciabatta.

4. Put on the baking sheet for the air fryer.

5. Depending on how you like your bread to taste, bake it in an air fryer that has been preheated at 370 °F for 3 to 5 minutes.

Potatoes Au Gratin

Time needed for prep: 10 minutes

Time needed to cook: 45 minutes

Serves: 2

Nutritional values per serving:

Calories: 341

Fat: 27 g

Carb: 20 g

Fiber Content: 1 g

Total Protein: 5 g

Ingredients:

- o half cup heavy whipping cream
- o 2 cloves garlic, peeled
- o half tbsp oil
- o Ground pepper as per taste
- o 1 small sweet potato, peeled, thinly sliced (about a ¾ cup)
- o 1 small russet potato, peeled, thinly sliced (about a ¾ cup)
- o 2 tbsps chopped onion
- o half tsp minced fresh thyme leaves
- o quarter tsp salt
- o 2 tbsps parmesan cheese (grated)
- o Cooking spray

Directions:

1. Spray some cooking spray on the baking accessory pan for the air fryer.

2. Fill a blender with cream, shallot, thyme, pepper, salt, onion, and garlic.

3. Blend until smooth, about 30 to 40 seconds.

4. Combine sweet and russet potatoes in a bowl. Pour some oil on it. Season with salt and pepper to taste. Well, toss.

5. Put the potato slices in the baking pan that has been prepared.

6. Place the potatoes on top of the mixed mixture.

7. Place the dish in the air fryer basket after covering it with aluminum foil.

8. Bake the potatoes for 30 to 40 minutes at 370 °F in an air fryer that has been preheated, or until they are practically soft.

9. Top with some Parmesan cheese. Dish should not be covered.

10. Increase the heat to 400 °F. Until the top is nicely golden brown, bake for 5 minutes.

11. Remove from the air fryer, then set aside for 5 minutes to rest.

12. Present hot.

Roasted Broccoli with Cheese Sauce

Time needed for prep: 15 minutes

Time needed to cook: 6–8 minutes

Serves: 2

Nutritional values per serving:

Calories: 108

Fat: 2 g

Carb: 15 g

Fiber Content: 4 g

Total Protein: 8 g

Ingredients:

- o   6 ounces broccoli florets
- o   5 tbsps low-fat evaporated milk
- o   2 tsps aji amarillo paste
- o   ¾ ounce queso fresco (Fresh Mexican cheese), crumbled
- o   3 low-sodium saltine crackers
- o   Cooking spray

Directions:

1. Fill a bowl with broccoli. Use cooking spray to spritz. Toss thoroughly and re-spray. Well, toss. Transfer to the basket of an air fryer.

2. Air-fry at 375 °F for 6 to 8 minutes, or until the food is crisp and tender.

3. In the meantime, combine the ingredients in a blender and purée until smooth. Put into a jar that can be microwaved.

4. For 20 to 30 seconds, raise the microwave's temperature. Stir thoroughly to mix.

5. Pour onto broccoli, then plate.

Roasted Asian Broccoli

Time needed for prep: 10 minutes

Time needed to cook: 20 minutes

Serves: 2

Nutritional values per serving:

Calories: 154

Fat: 11 g

Carb: 11 g

Fiber Content: 4 g

Total Protein: 6.5 g

Ingredients:

- o half pd broccoli, chop into florets
- o half tbsp crushed garlic
- o 1 tbsp soy sauce (low-sodium)
- o 1 tsp sriracha
- o 3 tbsps roasted, salted peanuts
- o ¾ tsp peanut oil
- o Salt as per taste
- o 1 tsp honey or agave nectar
- o half tsp rice vinegar
- o Lime juice (freshly squeezed) to drizzle (optional)
- o A large pinch sesame seeds to garnish (optional)

Directions:

1. Toss together the broccoli, garlic, and salt in a bowl.

2. Drizzle broccoli with peanut oil and toss until all of the broccoli is thoroughly covered.

3. Insert into the basket of an air fryer. It should be spread out in one layer.

4. Roast for 15-20 minutes, or until crisp and golden brown, in an air fryer that has been preheated to 375 °F. Incorporate into a bowl.

5. In the meantime, combine the ingredients in a microwave-safe bowl. For about 10 seconds, raise the temperature in the microwave. Combine thoroughly after mixing. Give the broccoli a pour. Well, toss.

6. Top with lime juice and peanuts before serving.

Chapter 12 - Pizzas and Pasta Recipes

Whole-Wheat Pita Pizzas

Time needed for prep: 10 minutes

Time needed to cook: 10 minutes

Serves: 1

Nutritional values per serving:

Calories: 229

Fat: 5 g

Carb: 37 g

Fiber Content: 5 g

Total Protein: 11 g

Ingredients:

- o 2 tbsps low-sodium marinara sauce
- o half cup spinach leaves (small)
- o half tsp sliced garlic
- o Shaved Parmigiano-Reggiano cheese
- o 1 whole-wheat pita round
- o 4 plum tomato slices
- o 2 tbsps shredded mozzarella

Directions:

1. Spread the pita bread with marinara sauce. Spread garlic and spinach leaves.

Slices of tomato are placed. grate some mozzarella cheese.

3. Sprinkle Parmigiano-Reggiano cheese shavings on top.

4. Put in the basket of the air fryer.

5. Bake for roughly 4-5 minutes at 360 °F in an air fryer that has been preheated.

6. Slice into wedges, then plate.

Deep-Dish Pepperoni Pizza

Time needed for prep: 10 minutes

Time needed to cook: 35 minutes

Serves: 2

Nutritional values per serving:

Calories: 410

Fat: 16 g

Carb: 50 g

Fiber Content: 1 g

Total Protein: 17 g

Ingredients:

- o   half can Pillsbury refrigerated classic pizza crust
- o   3 tbsps pizza sauce
- o   0.4 ounce pepperoni slices
- o   half tbsp olive oil
- o   half cup shredded mozzarella cheese
- o   1 tbsp shredded mozzarella cheese
- o   Cooking spray

Directions:

1. Unfold the pizza crust and form it into a roughly 6-7-inch circular. Place inside a little circular baking dish that has been parchment paper-lined (also grease the parchment paper with cooking spray).

2. Slightly press the dough against the dish's rims and the bottom of the basket.

3. Bake for roughly 10 minutes at 360 °F in an air fryer that has been preheated.

4. Dispense with the parchment paper and remove the crust from the pan.

5. Rub a little olive oil on the crust's top and sides.

6. Spread the sauce over the pizza crust. You can then top with some mozzarella cheese. After that, you must arrange the slices of pepperoni. Finally, sprinkle Parmesan cheese on top to complete the preparation.

7. Put in the basket of the air fryer.

8. Bake for 4 to 7 minutes, depending on your preference for doneness.

Eggplant Parmesan Mini Pizzas

Time needed for prep: 20 minutes

Time needed to cook: 10 minutes per batch

Serves: 16

Nutritional values per serving:

Calories: 178

Fat: 7.6 g

Carb: 16.4 g

Fiber Content: 3.4 g

Total Protein: 11.4 g

Ingredients:

- o 2 medium eggplants, chop into half-inch-thick round slices (you should have 16 slices in all)
- o 2 eggs, beaten

- 2 cups Italian bread crumbs
- 8 ounces pizza sauce
- 16 ounces mozzarella cheese, shredded
- Salt as per taste
- 2 tbsps water
- half cup freshly parmesan cheese (grated)
- 2 cans (2.25 ounces each) sliced ripe olives, drained
- 2 tbsps chopped fresh basil to garnish
- Cooking spray

Directions:

1. Sprinkle salt on both sides of the eggplant slices. Wait 10 minutes before moving.

2. Use paper towels to gently massage the eggplant slices dry.

3. In a bowl, combine bread crumbs and Parmesan cheese.

4. Arrange a foil sheet on a baking pan with a rim. Put a rack on top of it. Place aside.

5. Whisk well in the egg and water in a separate basin.

6. Start by drizzling eggplant slices with the egg mixture. Shake to remove any extra egg, then roll it in bread crumbs.

7. Spray some cooking spray on the air fryer basket to grease it. Make batches of food. Put the air fryer basket with the eggplant slices inside. Spray the eggplant slices with cooking spray liberally on top.

8. Air fried for 10 minutes at 400 °F in a preheated air fryer.

9. Take out the eggplant slices and set them on the ready-made rack.

10. While the remaining batches of eggplant slices are being cooked, keep the rack with the baking sheet warm in the oven.

11. Turn on the broiler setting on the oven and wait for it to warm up.

12. Cover the eggplant pieces with pizza sauce. Sprinkle mozzarella cheese and olives on top of it.

13. Broil the food for 4-5 minutes, or until the cheese melts and starts to turn a little bit brown.

14. Top with basil and then serve.

Margherita Pizza

Time needed for prep: 10 minutes

Time needed to cook: 10 minutes

Serves: 4

Nutritional values per serving:

Calories: 481

Fat: 20 g

Carb: 57 g

Fiber Content: 2 g

Total Protein: 19 g

Ingredients:

- 16 ounces prepared pizza dough, thaw if frozen
- half cup crushed tomatoes
- 2 ounces shredded Italian cheese blend
- 2 tbsps olive oil
- 4 ounce fresh mozzarella pearls or chopped into small pieces
- A handful fresh basil to garnish

Directions:

1. Separate the dough into two equal pieces. create balls out of.

2. Lightly dust your countertop with flour. Each section should be rolled out to a thickness of about 1/4 inch.

3. Oil the dough's top portion using a brush.

4. Cover it with tomatoes. Add mozzarella and an Italian cheese blend on top.

5. Use batch baking.

6. Put a pizza in the basket of the air fryer.

7. Bake for 6 to 8 minutes at 400 °F in a preheated air fryer to melt the cheese.

8. Sprinkle basil leaves over the top.

9. Slice into wedges, then plate.

Roasted Vegetable Pasta Salad

Time needed for prep: 30 minutes

Time needed to cook: 1 hour and 20 minutes

Serves: 8

Nutritional values per serving: (1 cup):

Calories: 121

Fat: 1.3 g

Carb: 23.9 g

Fiber Content: 5.3 g

Total Protein: 5.4 g

Ingredients:

- o   1 medium eggplant, chop into half-inch-thick rounds
- o   3 small zucchinis, chop into half-inch-thick rounds
- o   2 tomatoes, chop into ⅛-inch slices
- o   1 red or green bell pepper, chopped into one" squares
- o   2 cups dry large pasta
- o   2 tsps olive oil
- o   half cup halved cherry tomatoes
- o   4 tbsps grated Parmesan
- o   Handful of basil, chopped
- o   quarter cup low-fat Italian dressing
- o   1 tsp salt or to taste
- o   Pepper as per taste

Directions:

1. Set the air fryer's temperature to 350 °F and turn it on to warm up.

In a bowl, put the eggplant. Add a teaspoon of oil to it. Place in the air fryer basket after thoroughly mixing.

3. Roast until tender, about 20 to 30 minutes.

4. Remove from the basket, then place aside.

5. Include the zucchini in a bowl. Add a teaspoon of oil to it. Place in the air fryer basket after thoroughly mixing.

6. Air-fry until tender, which should take 20 to 30 minutes.

7. Remove from the basket, then place aside.

8. Fill the air fryer basket with tomatoes. Use cooking spray to spritz.

9. Cook it in the air fryer for 20 to 30 minutes, or until it starts to brown.

10. Remove from the basket, then place aside.

11. Prepare the pasta as directed in the meantime.

12. Drain and add to a dish of salad.

13. Fill the pasta bowl with the remaining ingredients and all of the roasted vegetables. After carefully folding, chill for a few hours.

14. While it chills, stir a couple of times.

15. Whether at room temperature or chilled, serve.

Mascarpone Mushroom Pasta

Time needed for prep: 10 minutes

Time needed to cook: 15 minutes

Serves: 2

Nutritional values per serving:

Calories: 402

Fat: 35 g

Carb: 10 g

Fiber Content: 1 g

Total Protein: 12 g

Ingredients:

- 2 cups sliced mushrooms
- 1 tsp crushed garlic
- 4 ounces mascarpone cheese, chopped
- half tsp pepper
- quarter tsp red pepper flakes
- half cup chopped onion
- 2 tbsps cream or half-and-half
- half tsp dried thyme
- half tsp salt
- quarter cup shredded cheese
- 2 cups pasta

Directions:

1. Spray cooking spray on the air fryer baking attachment.

2. In a bowl, combine the mushrooms, cream, mascarpone cheese, salt, pepper, thyme, and red pepper flakes. Stir to combine. Place inside the ready pan.

3. Bake for 10 to 15 minutes at 350 °F in an air fryer that has been preheated. Halfway through baking, stir once.

4. Prepare the pasta according to the package directions in the interim.

5. Add cooked pasta to a serving bowl. Add the mushroom mixture on top. After serving, top with cheese.

Air Fryer Ravioli

Time needed for prep: 10 minutes

Time needed to cook: 12 minutes

Serves: 3

Nutritional values per serving: (3 pieces):

Calories: 107

Fat: 3 g

Carb: 12 g

Fiber Content: 1 g

Total Protein: 5 g

Ingredients:

- o   1 small egg
- o   Cooking spray (optional)
- o   half cup marinara sauce, warmed, to serve
- o   9–10 mini cheese ravioli
- o   half cup freshly grated parmesan, plus 2 tsps extra for garnishing
- o   half cup bread crumbs (panko)
- o   2 tsps Italian seasoning

Directions:

1. Combine Parmesan, Italian seasoning, and bread crumbs (panko) in a bowl.

2. In a separate bowl, mix together the egg and the water.

3. Just before frying, remove the ravioli from the freezer. Initially, coat the ravioli in the egg. Shake to remove any extra egg, then roll it in the bread crumbs to coat. Put the ravioli in the basket of the air fryer. Spray the cooking spray all over it liberally.

4. Air-fry at 360 °F for 12 minutes, or until golden brown, in a preheated air fryer. Halfway through frying, flip the sides. Once the sides have been flipped, reapply some oil.

5. Top with Parmesan cheese and serve immediately with heated marinara.

Green Curry Noodles

Time needed for prep: 1 hour 15 minutes

Time needed to cook: 25 minutes

Serves: 3

Nutritional values per serving:

Calories: 271

Fat: 6.1 g

Carb: 32.7 g

Fiber Content: 8.6 g

Total Protein: 21.4 g

Ingredients:

- o   1 pd shirataki noodles
- o   ¾ tbsp fish sauce (optional)

- quarter tsp garlic powder
- 2.5 ounces snow peas
- 6 ounces tofu (extra-firm), cubed
- 2 ounces mushrooms, thinly sliced
- 1 small green bell pepper, thinly sliced
- 1 small red pepper or red peppers, thinly sliced
- half cup sliced water chestnuts
- 1 cup broccoli florets
- 6 ounces Napa cabbage
- 2 spring onions (finely sliced)
- 1 carrot, peeled, shredded
- half tsp ground fresh cilantro or 1 tsp cilantro (chopped)
- 1 tsp lemongrass paste
- 1half tbsps lime juice
- 2 tbsps rice vinegar
- 3 tbsps Thai green curry paste or red curry paste to taste
- half tsp sesame oil
- 4 tbsps soy sauce
- 6 large shrimp, cooked

Directions:

1. If the shirataki noodles are packaged with water, drain the water. Rinse under cool, flowing water. Place into a big basin. Add a half-tbsp of soy sauce and a cup of boiling water. Fork-mix, then set aside for a while.

2. Combine 1 1/2 tbsp of soy sauce, sesame oil, fish sauce, and garlic powder in a basin to marinade the tofu. Mix thoroughly after adding tofu.

3. Combine the rice vinegar, lime juice, ground cilantro paste, lemongrass paste, and 2 tablespoons of Thai curry paste in a bowl to make the dressing. Place aside.

4. Set a skillet on the medium heat. Spray the cooking spray all over it liberally. Add the broccoli, snow peas, mushrooms, peppers, and water chestnuts and sauté until cooked. Remove from heat, then place aside.

5. In a bowl, combine cabbage, carrots, and spring onions. Place aside.

6. Using a spoon, remove the tofu from the marinade. Place the tofu in the air fryer basket and set aside the marinade.

7. Use cooking spray to coat the tofu.

8. Air fried for 12 to 13 minutes at 360 °F in a preheated air fryer. While cooking, shake the basket a few times. Put aside after transferring to a bowl.

9. After that, add shrimp to the basket of the air fryer. Use cooking spray to spritz. For five minutes, cook. Halfway through cooking, flip the sides.

10. Heat a wok or skillet to medium heat to prepare the stir fry sauce. Thai curry paste, the remaining vinegar, and the tofu marinade that was saved. Stir thoroughly to mix. Stir-fry for 2-3 minutes after adding the cabbage mixture. Remove from the heat.

11. Place the drained noodles in a big bowl. Dressing is poured on top. Include vegetables and tofu. Over it, drizzle the stir-fried sauce. Use a pair of tongs toss.

12. Add shrimp on top before serving.

Chapter 13 - Desserts

Nutella S'mores

Time needed for prep: 2 minutes

Time needed to cook: 5 minutes

Serves: 2

Nutritional values per serving:

Calories: 172

Fat: 2 g

Carb: 35 g

Fiber Content: 0 g

Total Protein: 1 g

Ingredients:

- o   2 graham crackers, halved
- o   A few strawberries or raspberries
- o   2 large marshmallows
- o   2 tsps Nutella

Directions:

2 Graham crackers should be placed in the air fryer basket.

2. Top each cracker with a marshmallow.

3. Bake for 5 to 6 minutes, or until the marshmallow is golden brown, in an air fryer that has been preheated to 350 °F.

4. Sprinkle some berries on top of the marshmallow. Add a tablespoon of Nutella to the berries.

5. Finish by placing the remaining graham cracker halves on top, then serve.

Chocolate Cake

Time needed for prep: 10 minutes

Time needed to cook: 15 minutes

Serves: 8

Nutritional values per serving:

Calories: 214

Fat: 11.7 g

Carb: 25.5 g

Fiber Content: 0.8 g

Total Protein: 3.2 g

Ingredients:

- o   half cup white sugar
- o   2 eggs
- o   ¾ flour (all purpose)
- o   2 tbsps cocoa powder
- o   7 tbsps unsalted butter
- o   quarter tsp salt
- o   2 tbsps apricot jam
- o   half tsp baking powder
- o   Cooking spray

Directions:

1. Combine the butter and sugar, then beat at a medium-high speed with an electric mixer until it is light and fluffy.

2. Reduce the speed to medium, add each egg separately, and beat thoroughly after each addition.

3. Combine all the dry ingredients in a bowl.

4. Add a small amount at a time, stirring thoroughly after each addition to the mixing bowl.

5. Spoon the batter into an air fryer-compatible cake pan that has been buttered.

6. Insert the pan into the basket of the air fryer.

7. Bake for 10 to 15 minutes at 320 °F in an air fryer that has been preheated, or until a knife inserted in the center of the cake comes out clean. Before the timer goes off, do not open the air fryer.

8. Take out the air fryer pan and let it cool.

9. Carefully remove the cake from the plate by cutting all the way around its edges.

10. Cut and present.

Cinnamon Apple Chips with Almond Yogurt Dip

Time needed for prep: 10 minutes

Time needed to cook: 12 minutes per batch

Serves: 8

Nutritional values per serving: (6–8 chips with 1 tbsp dip):

Calories: 104

Fat: 3 g

Carb: 17 g

Fiber Content: 3 g

Total Protein: 1 g

Ingredients:

- 2 apples like Fuji or Honeycrisp, thinly sliced with a mandolin slicer
- 4 tsps canola oil
- 2 tsps cinnamon powder
- Cooking spray
- For the dip:
- 2 tbsps almond butter
- half cup plain 1% low-fat Yogurt (Greek)
- 2 tsps honey

Directions:

In a bowl, add apple slices. Add some cinnamon to it. Pour oil over the food and toss to evenly coat.

2. Spray some cooking spray on the air fryer basket. Make batches of food.

3. Stacking or overlapping the apple slices is not allowed in the air fryer basket.

4. Fry for 12 minutes at 375 °F in an air fryer that has been preheated. After every 4 minutes, switch the sides. Flip the sides over, then flatten them. The chips might not be crisp when the timer goes off.

5. Remove from the air fryer and allow to fully cool. By now, the chips should be crunchy.

6. To assemble the dip, mix all of the required ingredients in a bowl and whisk to incorporate.

7. Provide dip and apple chips.

Chocolate Chip Oatmeal Cookies

Time needed for prep: 20 minutes

Time needed to cook: 10 minutes per batch

Serves: 3 dozen

Nutritional values per serving: (1 cookie):

Calories: 102

Fat: 5 g

Carb: 13 g

Fiber Content: 1 g

Total Protein: 2 g

Ingredients:

- o   half cup butter, softened
- o   6 tbsps packed brown sugar
- o   6 tbsps sugar

- half tsp vanilla extract
- ¾ cup flour (all purpose)
- 1half cups quick cooking oats
- half package (from a 3.4 ounce package) pudding mix (vanilla)
- half tsp salt
- half cup chopped nuts
- 1 egg
- half tsp baking soda
- 1 cup chocolate chips

Directions:

1. Combine the butter and sugar, then beat at a medium-high speed with an electric mixer until it is light and fluffy.

2. Reduce the speed to medium, add each egg separately, and beat thoroughly after each addition.

3. Combine all the dry ingredients in a bowl.

4. Insert into the butter basin. Mix until completely combined.

5. Stir in the nuts and chocolate chips.

6. Divide the mixture into little balls, then flatten each one. batches when baking.

7. Use foil to line the air fryer basket. In the air fryer, put the cookies. Place space between each biscuit.

8. Bake for 8 to 10 minutes, or until light brown, in an air fryer that has been preheated to 350 °F.

Banana Bread / Banana Muffins

Time needed for prep: 15 minutes

Time needed to cook: 30 minutes

Serves: 4

Nutritional values per serving:

Calories: 180

Fat: 6 g

Carb: 29 g

Fiber Content: 2 g

Total Protein: 4 g

Ingredients:

- o 6 tbsps white whole-wheat flour
- o quarter tsp salt
- o 1 medium very ripe banana, mashed
- o quarter cup sugar
- o 1 tbsp vegetable oil
- o 1 tbsp chopped walnuts
- o ⅛ tsp baking soda
- o 1 egg, lightly beaten
- o half tsp cinnamon powder
- o half tsp vanilla extract
- o 3 tbsps nonfat yogurt

Directions:

1. In a mixing basin, sift the flour, baking soda, salt, and cinnamon.

2. In a bowl, whisk together the egg, yogurt, banana, oil, sugar, and vanilla.

3. Add the banana mixture to the bowl with the dry ingredients and well stir.

4. To prepare banana bread, lightly grease a small loaf pan (that fits comfortably inside the air fryer basket). Put the bread in the prepared batter. Spread uniformly.

5. Cover the batter with walnuts entirely.

6. Insert the air fryer basket into the loaf pan.

7. Bake in an air fryer that has been preheated to 350 °F or until a toothpick inserted in the center comes out clean.

8. When finished, remove from the air fryer and let cool. Place the loaf on a wire rack to cool entirely after being removed from the pan.

9. Cut and plate.

Strawberry "Pop Tarts"

Time needed for prep: 70-80 minutes

Time needed to cook: 10 minutes

Serves: 12

Nutritional values per serving:

Calories: 229

Fat: 9 g

Carb: 39 g

Fiber Content: 1 g

Total Protein: 2 g

Ingredients:

- o   16 ounces strawberries, quartered
- o   1 package (14.1 ounces) refrigerated piecrusts
- o   1 cup powdered sugar
- o   half cup granulated sugar
- o   1 ounce rainbow candy sprinkles

Directions:

1. Put strawberries in a microwave-safe bowl. Stir in the granulated sugar. Stir every five minutes while letting the mixture sit for about 10-15 minutes.

2. Ten minutes or so in the microwave. While cooking, stir a couple of times. Make sure it reaches room temperature.

3. Lightly dust your countertop with flour.

4. Cover it with the piecrust dough and roll it. 24 2.5 x 3 inch rectangles should be cut. Roll any leftover dough again.

5. Center 12 of the rectangles with about 2 tsp of the strawberry filling. Place away from the edges (leave about half inch all along the edges).

6. Water the rectangles' edges all over with a brush.

7. Cover these rectangles with the remaining 12 rectangles. For a good design, seal the edges by pressing it down with a fork.

8. Coat the tarts with cooking spray. batches when baking. When baking, avoid overlapping.

9. Bake for 10 minutes, or until golden brown, in an air fryer that has been preheated to 350 °F.

10. Take out and set on a wire rack after air fryer. Wait until it reaches room temperature.

11. In the meantime, combine the powdered sugar and lime juice in a basin.

12. Place this mixture on top of the tarts. Serve with sprinkling of rainbow-colored confectionery.

Churros with Chocolate Sauce

Time needed for prep: 60 minutes

Time needed to cook: 10 minutes per batch

Serves: 6

Nutritional values per serving: (2 churros with 2 tsps chocolate sauce):

Calories: 173

Fat: 11 g

Carb: 12 g

Fiber Content: 1 g

Total Protein: 3 g

Ingredients:

quarter cup water

- o   3 tbsps unsalted butter, divided
- o   1 egg
- o   1 tsp cinnamon powder
- o   1half tbsps heavy cream
- o   ⅛ tsp kosher salt
- o   quarter cup flour (all purpose)
- o   3 tbsps granulated sugar
- o   2 ounces bittersweet baking chocolate, chopped
- o   1 tbsp vanilla kefir

Directions:

1. Fill a small saucepan with water, 2 tablespoons of butter, and salt. Set the saucepan's heat to medium-high.

2. Reduce the heat to medium-low after it starts to boil.

3. Add the flour and stir. Stir continuously until thoroughly combined and lump-free.

4. Continue stirring until the dough begins to pull away from the pan's sides. It shouldn't take longer than 2-3 minutes to do this.

5. Turn off the heat. Into a bowl, spoon. Stir continuously for a few minutes.

6. Add the egg and continue to whisk until well integrated.

7. Pour the mixture into a piping bag and attach a star-tipped nozzle to it. Place for 30 minutes in the refrigerator.

8. Use batch cooking.

9. In the air fryer basket, pipe into 3-inch-long sections.

10. Fry for 10 minutes, or until golden brown, in an air fryer that has been preheated to 350 °F.

11. Fill a basin with sugar and cinnamon.

12. Spread the churros with the remaining butter. the sugar mixture and dredge.

13. In the meantime, combine chocolate and heavy cream in a microwave-safe small bowl.

14. For 30 seconds, raise the microwave's temperature. halfway through cooking, stir once.

15. Stir in kefir well.

16. Provide chocolate dip for churros.

Doughnuts

Time needed for prep: 60-70 minutes

Time needed to cook: 10 minutes per batch

Serves: 16

Nutritional values per serving:

Calories: 238

Fat: 4 g

Carb: 46 g

Fiber Content: 1 g

Total Protein: 5 g

Ingredients:

o   half cup warm water (100-110 °F)

- o   half cup, plus 1 tsp granulated white sugar
- o   half tsp salt
- o   4 tbsps unsalted butter, melted
- o   2 tsps active dry yeast
- o   4 cups flour (all purpose)
- o   half cup milk at room temperature
- o   2 large eggs, beaten
- o   For the glaze:
- o   8 tsps water
- o   2 cups powdered sugar

Directions:

1. In a bowl, combine yeast, water, and 1 tsp of granulated sugar. Stir. Set aside until foamy for 5 to 8 minutes.

2. In a mixing basin, combine the remaining sugar, flour, and salt.

3. Add the milk, eggs, butter, and yeast mixture. Use a wooden spoon to stir until a soft dough forms.

4. Sprinkle some flour on your countertop. Till the dough is smooth, knead it.

5. Transfer the dough to a greased bowl. Wait until it doubles in size while keeping it covered in a warm environment. It ought should take an hour or so.

6. Lightly dust your countertop with flour. The dough should be rolled out to a thickness of 1/4 inch.

7. Use a doughnut cutter to cut into doughnuts.

8. Gather the leftover dough, reroll it, and cut it into doughnuts. 16 doughnuts should be ordered.

9. Lightly dust your countertop with flour. Donuts should be placed on the floured surface. Make a loose tent out of plastic foil. Continue to let it grow until it doubles in size.

10. Put in the basket of the air fryer. batches when baking.

11. Bake for 5-8 minutes, or until golden brown, in an air fryer that has been preheated to 350 °F.

12. Place a baking sheet on top of a wire rack.

13. In a bowl, combine water and powdered sugar to make the glaze.

14. After dipping the doughnuts in the glaze, shake them to remove any extra glaze. affix to the rack. In a little while, the glaze will become firm.

15. Deliver according to your preferences

Peach Pies

Time needed for prep: 20 minutes

Time needed to cook: 12-14 minutes per batch

Serves: 4

Nutritional values per serving: (1 pie):

Calories: 314

Fat: 16 g

Carb: 43 g

Fiber Content: 1 g

Total Protein: 3 g

Ingredients:

- o   1 fresh peach of about 5 ounces, peeled, pitted, chopped
- o   1half tbsps granulated sugar
- o   A pinch table salt
- o   half package (from a 14.1-ounce package) refrigerated piecrusts
- o   half tbsp fresh lime juice
- o   half tsp vanilla extract
- o   half tsp cornflour
- o   Cooking spray

Directions:

1. In a bowl, combine the peach, sugar, salt, lime juice, and vanilla. Set aside for ten to fifteen minutes. Every five minutes, stir.

2. Drain out the peach's leftover liquid, saving roughly half a tablespoon of it.

3. Stir the cornflour into the liquid that has been retained. Pour into the peach basin. Mix thoroughly.

4. Use the piecrust to cut four-inch circles. There should be a total of 4 circles.

5. Split the filling in half and spread each circle's half with it. Over the filling, secure the second half. The pies are shaped like a semicircle. With a fork, press to seal the edges. Create 3 little cuts in the tops of each pie.

6. Use cooking spray to coat the pies before placing them in the air fryer. If necessary, cook in batches. Avoid overlapping.

7. Fry for 12 to 14 minutes, or until golden brown, in an air fryer that has been preheated to 350 °F.

8. Serve in the manner of your choice

Double-Glazed Cinnamon Biscuit Bites

Time needed for prep: 25 minutes

Time needed to cook: 15 minutes

Serves: 4

Nutritional values per serving: (2 bites):

Calories: 325

Fat: 7 g

Carb: 60 g

Fiber Content: 5 g

Total Protein: 8 g

Ingredients:

- o ⅓ cup whole-wheat flour
- o ⅓ cup flour (all purpose)
- o 1 tbsp granulated sugar
- o ⅛ tsp cinnamon powder, plus extra to garnish
- o 2 tbsps cold salted butter, chop into small pieces
- o half tsp baking powder
- o A pinch kosher salt
- o 3 tbsps whole milk
- o Cooking spray
- o For glaze:
- o 3–4 tsps water
- o 1 cup powdered sugar

Directions:

1. Combine all the dry ingredients for the biscuit bits in a bowl and whisk. Using a pastry cutter or a pair of knives, incorporate butter into the mixture until coarse crumbs form.

2. To create dough, add the milk and stir.

3. Lightly dust your countertop. On the floured surface, knead the dough for 30 to 40 seconds, or until it is smooth.

4. Make balls out of the dough by dividing it into 8 equal pieces.

5. Spray cooking spray in the basket of the air fryer. The balls should be put in the air fryer. Between each biscuit, leave a space. If necessary, cook in batches.

6. Bake for 10 to 12 minutes, or until golden brown, in an air fryer that has been preheated to 350 °F. They too would have inflated.

7. Place a baking sheet on top of a wire rack. Place the biscuit bits on the wire rack after removing them from the air fryer. 4 to 5 minutes of cooling.

8. In a bowl, combine powdered sugar and water to make the glaze.

9. Cover the biscuit bites with the glaze. In a little while, the glaze will become firm. Put another glaze layer on top of it. Allow it to cool for a while.

10. Deliver according to your preferences

Chapter 14 – Air Fryer Breakfast Recipes

Blueberry Muffins (Gluten-Free)

Time needed for prep: 15 minutes

Time needed to cook: 10 minutes

Serves: 7

Nutritional values per serving:

Calories: 201

Fat: 8.8

Carb: 27.3 g

Fiber Content: 1.2 g

Total Protein: 2.9 g

Ingredients:

- o   half cup frozen blueberries
- o   3 tbsps coconut sugar

- o 1 tsp baking powder
- o 1 small egg
- o half tsp vanilla extract
- o half cup cassava flour or any other gluten-free flour of your choice
- o quarter tsp salt
- o 2 tbsps unsweetened applesauce
- o 2 tbsps melted ghee or coconut oil
- o 2 tbsps unsweetened almond milk

Directions:

1. Spray cooking spray on a silicone muffin pan.

2. In a mixing basin, combine the blueberries, coconut sugar, baking soda, cassava flour, and salt.

3. In a another bowl, combine applesauce, ghee, milk, egg, and vanilla.

4. Pour the blueberry mixture into the bowl. Mix until completely combined.

5. Spoon the batter evenly among the muffin cups. Put the object in the air fryer tray. baking in batches as necessary.

6. Bake for 10 minutes at 360 °F in an air fryer that has been preheated. Place the muffin tin on a cooling rack after removing it from the air fryer.

7. Serve in the manner of your choice

Breakfast Frittata

Time needed for prep: 15 minutes

Time needed to cook: 20 minutes

Serves: 4

Nutritional values per serving:

Calories: 380

Fat: 27.4 g

Carb: 2.9 g

Fiber Content: 0.4 g

Total Protein: 31.2 g

Ingredients:

- o   quarter cup diced red peppers
- o   8 eggs, lightly beaten
- o   A pinch cayenne pepper
- o   1 cup shredded Monterey Jack cheese
- o   half pd breakfast sausage, cooked, crumbled
- o   Salt as per taste
- o   Pepper as per taste
- o   2 green onions (finely sliced)

Directions:

1. In a bowl, combine the eggs, cheese, sausage, bell pepper, green onion, salt, pepper, and cayenne pepper. Whisk thoroughly.

2. Spray some cooking spray on the air fryer baking attachment. In the baking tool, uniformly distribute the mixture. The egg mixture should be spread out. Distribute it evenly.

3. Bake for 18 to 20 minutes at 360 °F in a preheated air fryer.

4. Cut into four wedges, then serve.

Breakfast Potatoes in the Air Fryer

Time needed for prep: 2 minutes

Time needed to cook: 15 minutes

Serves: 6

Nutritional values per serving:

Calories: 375

Fat: 7 g

Carb: 67 g

Fiber Content: 13 g

Total Protein: 13 g

Ingredients:

- o   2 tbsps oil

- o 10 medium Yukon gold potatoes, peeled, chopped into one" cubes
- o Cooking spray
- o For potato seasoning:
- o 1 tsp smoked paprika
- o half tsp pepper
- o 1 tsp kosher salt
- o 1 tsp garlic powder

Directions:

1. Fill a container with potatoes.

2. Fill a small bowl with the complete ingredient list for the potato seasoning, then whisk. Over the potatoes, sprinkle. Well, toss.

3. Add oil to it and give it a good toss.

4. Spray some cooking spray on the air fryer basket to grease it.

5. Place the potatoes in the basket of the air fryer. If necessary, cook in batches.

6. Bake for 10 to 15 minutes at 400 °F in an air fryer that has been preheated, or until fully cooked and browned. Every three to four minutes, shake the basket.

7. Present hot.

Cheese and Veggie Egg Cups

Time needed for prep: 10 minutes

Time needed to cook: 20 minutes

Serves: 2

Nutritional values per serving:

Calories: 195

Fat: 12 g

Carb: 7 g

Fiber Content: 1 g

Total Protein: 13 g

Ingredients:

- o 2 large eggs
- o half cup shredded cheese
- o half tbsp cilantro (chopped)
- o half cup diced vegetables of your choice
- o 2 tbsps half-and-half
- o Salt as per taste
- o Pepper as per taste
- o Cooking spray

Directions:

1. Spray some cooking spray on two ramekins to grease them.

2. Whisk the eggs thoroughly in a bowl. Stir thoroughly after adding the half-and-half, cheese, cilantro, salt, and pepper.

3. Place ramekins with a spoon. Put them in the basket of the air fryer.

4. Bake for 12 minutes at 300 °F in an air fryer that has been preheated.

5. Top each ramekin with 2 tbsp. of cheese.

6. Increase the air fryer's temperature to 400 °F and bake the food for 2 minutes, or until the top is lightly browned.

7. Serve immediately.

Air-Fried Potato Hash

Time needed for prep: 15 minutes

Time needed to cook: 40 minutes

Serves: 2

Nutritional values per serving: (1 cup):

Calories: 199

Fat: 2.4 g

Carb: 34.4 g

Fiber Content: 5.5 g

Total Protein: 10.4 g

Ingredients:

- ¾ pd potatoes, rinsed, chopped into small cubes
- 1 onion, chopped
- half cup egg substitute or 2 large eggs
- 1 small green bell pepper, chopped
- quarter tsp dried thyme
- quarter tsp dried savory
- 1 tsp duck fat
- Salt as per taste
- Ground pepper as per taste
- Cooking spray

Directions:

1. Bell pepper, onion, and lard should be added to the air fryer basket.
2. 5 minutes at 350 °F or until onions are transparent.
3. Stir in the potatoes, salt, pepper, savory, and thyme.
4. Cook potatoes in an air fryer that has been preheated at 350 °F for 15 to 20 minutes, or until they are soft.
5. Put a pan on a moderately low heat in the meanwhile. Use cooking spray to spritz.
6. Pepper should be liberally applied to the pan. Keep it in the pan until it begins to smell. Cook the egg substitute until set after adding it.
7. On your chopping board, remove the cooked egg. Once it is safe to handle, slice it into pieces.
8. Add the egg pieces to the air fryer and stir when the allotted cooking time has passed.
9. For 4-5 minutes, air fry.
10. Serve warm.

Toasted Sandwich

Time needed for prep: 5 minutes

Time needed to cook: 7 minutes per sandwich

Serves: 2

Nutritional values per serving:

Calories: 297

Fat: 9.8 g

Carb: 27.7 g

Fiber Content: 4.1 g

Total Protein: 20.9 g

Ingredients:

- o   4 slices bread
- o   2 slices ham
- o   2 cheese slices
- o   2.1 ounces butter
- o   4 tomato slices

Directions:

1. Grab two slices of bread. Over each, place a slice of ham, cheese, and tomato. Add the final two slices of bread to form a covering.

2. Grill for 3-4 minutes at 390 °F in an air fryer that has been preheated. Cook the opposite side for 4 minutes after flipping the sides.

Chapter 15 - Air Fryer Appetizers/Snacks

Vegan Cheesy Potato Wedges

Time needed for prep: 10 minutes

Time needed to cook: 16 minutes

Serves: 2

Nutritional values per serving:

Calories: 220

Fat: 8 g

Carb: 30 g

Fiber Content: 4 g

Total Protein: 7.5 g

Ingredients:

For potatoes:

- half pd fingerling potatoes, chop into wedges
- half tsp kosher salt
- quarter tsp garlic powder
- half tsp extra-virgin olive oil
- Pepper as per taste
- For the cheese sauce:
- quarter cup raw cashews
- quarter tsp paprika
- half tsp fresh lime juice
- quarter tsp ground turmeric
- 1 tbsp nutritional yeast
- 1–2 tbsps water
- To garnish:
- Sliced green onion (optional)

Directions:

1. Fill a container with potatoes. Pour some oil on it. Garlic powder, pepper, and salt should all be added.

2. Put the potatoes in the basket of the air fryer.

3. Air-fry for 16 minutes, or until golden brown and thoroughly cooked, in a preheated air fryer at 400 °F.

4. While the basket is frying, shake it a few times.

5. In the meantime, combine the ingredients in a blender and process until smooth.

6. Spread the potatoes in the air fryer baking attachment after they are finished cooking.

7. Top the potato wedges with the cheese sauce.

8. Bake for 2 minutes at 400 °F in an air fryer that has been preheated.

9. Serve immediately.

Mexican-Style Corn on the Cob

Time needed for prep: 2 minutes

Time needed to cook: 14 minutes

Serves: 2

Nutritional values per serving: (1 ear corn):

Calories: 201

Fat: 7 g

Carb: 35 g

Fiber Content: 4 g

Total Protein: 6 g

Ingredients:

- o 2 ears fresh corn, shucked
- o 2 tsps unsalted butter
- o half tsp grated lime zest
- o half tbsp lime juice (freshly squeezed)
- o Pepper as per taste
- o Salt as per taste
- o 1 tbsp chopped fresh cilantro
- o 1 tsp crushed garlic
- o Cooking spray

Directions:

1. Use cooking spray to coat the corn cobs.

2. Roast for 14 minutes at 400 °F in an air fryer that has been preheated. During cooking, the corn should be turned a few times.

3. In a small microwave-safe bowl, combine the following ingredients: garlic, butter, lime juice, and lime zest. For around 30 to 40 seconds, raise the microwave's temperature until butter melts and garlic begins to smell good.

4. Arrange the corn cobs on a dish. Over it, drizzle the butter mixture. Season with salt and pepper. Serve with cilantro as a garnish.

Spanakopita Bites

Time needed for prep: 20 minutes

Time needed to cook: 12 minutes

Serves: 4

Nutritional values per serving: (2):

Calories: 82

Fat: 4 g

Carb: 7 g

Fiber Content: 1 g

Total Protein: 4 g

Ingredients:

- 5 ounces spinach leaves (small)
- 2 tbsps 1% low-fat cottage cheese
- 1 tbsp finely parmesan cheese (grated)
- Zest of half lemon
- Pepper as per taste
- A pinch cayenne pepper
- half tbsp olive oil
- 1 tbsp water
- 2 tbsp crumbled feta cheese
- 1 small egg white
- half tsp oregano herbs (dry)
- Kosher salt as per taste
- 2 sheets frozen filo dough (13×18 inches), thawed

Directions:

1. Heat a container that contains water to a high temperature. Add the spinach when it starts to boil, and cook it until it wilts. Place in a colander after draining. Remove any extra moisture from the spinach and store it in a container.

2. Combine the spinach in a bowl with the various varieties of cheese, lemon zest, pepper, cayenne pepper, water, egg white, oregano, and salt.

3. Arrange sheets of filo on your countertop. Each filo sheet is divided by two rectangles.

4. Apply oil to a single piece. Put another filo square on top of it. Brush once more with oil. Once you have four layers of filo, keep doing this.

5. Now, cut the filo layers into 4 strips, each measuring about 2 1/4 inches wide along the length. Then, crosswise divide each strip into two equal pieces. You now have a total of 8 strips.

6. In the shape of a triangle, place a small amount of the spinach mixture on one corner of the strip. Form a triangle by folding the filling corner. Fold once more in a zigzag pattern to form a triangle. Continue creating the triangle until the entire strip has been used. The final edge should be wetted, then firmly pressed. You will receive one triangle for each strip.

7. Continue with the additional strips. There should be a total of 8 filled triangles.

8. Apply cooking spray on the triangles. Make batches of food.

9. Fill the air fryer basket with four to five triangles.

10. Bake for 10 to 12 minutes at 390 °F or until golden brown in an air fryer that has been preheated. Halfway through baking, flip the sides.

11. Whether it's hot, warm, or room temperature, serve.

Falafels

Time needed for prep: 15 minutes

Time needed to cook: 15 minutes

Serves: 2

Nutritional values per serving: (3 falafels):

Calories: 216

Fat: 7 g

Carb: 31 g

Fiber Content: 9 g

Total Protein: 10 g

Ingredients:

o half cup dried chickpeas, soaked in water overnight, drained

- o 1 very small onion, chopped
- o half tbsp extra-virgin olive oil
- o 1 clove garlic, minced
- o quarter tsp chili powder (optional)
- o half tsp salt or to taste
- o half tbsp cumin powder
- o ⅛ tsp baking soda
- o half tbsp lime juice
- o quarter cup packed fresh parsley, minced
- o 1-2 tbsps water
- o Cooking spray

Directions:

1. Fill the food processor bowl with the chickpeas, onion, garlic, parsley, chili powder, salt, cumin, and baking soda. Process until the ingredients are finely crushed.

Move into a bowl in step two. Add. Mix thoroughly.

3. Separate into 8-9 balls, then form into patties. For making patties, you can oil your hands.

4. Apply a thin layer of oil to aluminum foil.

5. Fill the air fryer basket with the foil. Falafels should be put in the air fryer basket.

6. Air-fry the food for 10 to 15 minutes, or until golden, in a preheated air fryer at 375 °F.

7. Serve hot with your preferred dip.

8. For a full supper, you may also create larger patties and serve them with toppings of your choosing over buns or in pita bread.

Air Fryer Sweet Potato Chips

Time needed for prep: 5 minutes

Time needed to cook: 15 minutes

Serves: 2

Nutritional values per serving: (about 15 chips):

Calories: 60

Fat: 3.5 g

Carb: 7 g

Fiber Content: 1 g

Total Protein: 1 g

Ingredients:

- o 1 sweet potato, chop into ⅛-inch-thick slices
- o Sea salt as per taste
- o half tsp chopped fresh rosemary (optional)
- o half tbsp canola oil
- o Ground pepper as per taste
- o Cooking spray

Directions:

1. For 20 minutes, soak the sweet potato slices in a dish of cool water. To dry, drain and use a kitchen towel.

2. Put the slices of sweet potato in a basin and add oil to it. Well, toss. Salt, garlic powder, and rosemary should be added.

3. Put the sweet potatoes in the basket of the air fryer.

4. Air-fry at 350 °F for 14–15 minutes, or until golden and crisp, in a preheated air fryer.

5. While the basket is frying, shake it a few times.

6. Remove from the air fryer and allow to fully cool.

7. Either serve immediately or place in an airtight container. It may persist for 3 to 4 days.

Potato Chips

Time needed for prep: 30 minutes

Time needed to cook: 30 minutes

Serves: 2

Nutritional values per serving: (12 chips):

Calories: 100

Fat: 3.5 g

Carb: 15 g

Fiber Content: 1 g

Total Protein: 2 g

Ingredients:

- o 1 potato (about 7 ounces), rinsed, unpeeled, sliced into ⅛-inch thin slices using a slicer
- o Freshly pepper powder as per taste
- o half tbsp olive or canola oil
- o Salt as per taste

Directions:

1. Use cold water to rinse the potatoes. For around 15 minutes, soak the potato slices in a bowl of cold water. The potatoes should be drained and spread out in a single layer on a kitchen towel to dry. With paper towels, pat the chip's top.

2. Put the chips in a dish of dry water. Toss it thoroughly after adding oil. Toss thoroughly after adding salt and pepper. Spray cooking spray liberally within the air fryer basket. Insert the air fryer basket with the chips.

3. Air-fry at 375 °F for 20 to 30 minutes, or until the food is crisp. While cooking, shake the basket a few times.

4. If wanted, serve chips with a dip of your choice.

Roasted Curry Chickpeas

Time needed for prep: 5 minutes

Time needed to cook: 35–40 minutes

Serves: 2

Nutritional values per serving:

Calories: 173

Fat: 8 g

Carb: 18 g

Fiber Content: 5 g

Total Protein: 7 g

Ingredients:

- half can (from a 15.5-ounce can) garbanzo beans, drained, rinsed
- Salt as per taste
- 1 tbsp olive oil
- quarter tsp ground turmeric
- $\frac{1}{8}$ tsp cumin powder
- quarter tsp Aleppo pepper
- 1 tbsp red wine vinegar
- 1 tsp curry powder
- $\frac{1}{8}$ tsp coriander powder
- quarter tsp cinnamon powder
- Thinly sliced fresh cilantro

Directions:

1. Fill the air fryer baking attachment with garbanzo beans. Put some paper towels on top of it, then pat them dry.

2. Use the air fryer to cook the food.

3. Roast for about 20 minutes at 375 °F in an air fryer that has been preheated. About halfway through roasting, shake the dish.

4. Add salt, all the spices, excluding Aleppo pepper, and stir thoroughly when the cooking time is up. Olive oil should be applied to it. Well, toss.

5. Use the air fryer to cook the food.

6. Continue to roast for an additional 15 to 20 minutes, or until golden. About halfway through roasting, shake the dish.

7. Remove from the air fryer and allow to fully cool.

8. Add cilantro and Aleppo pepper for garnish before serving.

Beet Chips

Time needed for prep: 10 minutes

Time needed to cook: 25-30 minutes

Serves: 2

Nutritional values per serving: (1 cup)

Calories: 47

Fat: 2 g

Carb: 6 g

Fiber Content: 2 g

Total Protein: 1 g

Ingredients:

- o   ¾ pd red beets, peeled, chop into ⅛-inch-thick slices
- o   Kosher salt as per taste
- o   1 tsp canola oil
- o   Pepper as per taste

Directions:

1. Put beet chips in a serving dish. Toss it thoroughly after adding oil. Toss thoroughly after adding salt and pepper. Spray cooking spray liberally within the air fryer basket. Insert the air fryer basket with the chips.

2. Air-fry for 20 to 30 minutes, or until crisp, at 375 °F in a preheated air fryer. While cooking, shake the basket every five minutes.

3. After fully cooling, serve.

Kale Chips

Time needed for prep: 10 minutes

Time needed to cook: 6 minutes

Serves: 1

Nutritional values per serving:

Calories: 159

Fat: 8 g

Carb: 20 g

Fiber Content: 5 g

Total Protein: 7 g

Ingredients:

- o 3 cups packed, torn lacinato kale leaves, discard stems and ribs, rinsed, pat dried completely
- o half tsp soy sauce (low-sodium)
- o quarter tsp dried crushed garlic
- o half tbsp olive oil
- o half tsp sesame seeds
- o ⅛ tsp poppy seeds

Directions:

1. Fill a bowl with greens. Over it, drizzle some soy sauce and oil. Well, toss. With your fingertips, lightly rubbed the leaves.

2. Transfer to the basket of the air fryer.

3. Air-fry for about 6 minutes, or until crisp, in an air fryer that has been preheated to 375 °F. Halfway through the frying process, shake the basket.

4. Place on an oven sheet. Sprinkle poppy and sesame seeds over the hot chips.

5. After fully cooling, serve.

Bow Tie Pasta Chips

Time needed for prep: 30 minutes

Time needed to cook: 10 minutes

Serves: 1

Nutritional values per serving:

Calories: 294

Fat: 8 g

Carb: 49 g

Fiber Content: 2 g

Total Protein: 10 g

Ingredients:

- o   1 cup dry whole-wheat bow tie pasta
- o   half tbsp nutritional yeast
- o   quarter tsp salt
- o   half tbsp olive oil
- o   1 tsp Seasoning powder (Italian)
- o   Cooking spray

Directions:

1. Prepare the pasta according to the package's instructions, but cook it for only half as long. Drain and place in a container.

2. Add some olive oil and thoroughly stir.

3. Add Italian spice, salt, and nutritional yeast.

4. Spray the air fryer basket with cooking spray liberally. In the basket, spread out the pasta.

5. Air-fry at 390 °F for about 9 to 10 minutes, or until the food is crisp. Halfway through the frying process, shake the basket.

6. After fully cooling, serve.

Chapter 16 – Turkey Recipes

Air Fryer Turkey Bacon

Time needed for prep: 5 minutes

Time needed to cook: 30 minutes

Serves: 4

Nutritional values per serving: (1 slice):

Calories: 30

Fat: 1.5 g

Carb: 0 g

Fiber Content: 0 g

Total Protein: 6 g

Ingredients:

- 4 ounces uncured turkey bacon slices, halved

Directions:

1. Put the pieces of turkey bacon in the basket of the air fryer.

2. Air-fry at 360 °F for 10 minutes, or until the desired doneness, in an air fryer that has been preheated. Halfway through frying, flip the sides.

Italian Meatballs

Time needed for prep: 20 minutes

Time needed to cook: 12 minutes

Serves: 6

Nutritional values per serving: (2 meatballs, without sauce)

Calories: 122

Fat: 0 g

Carb: 0 g

Fiber Content: 0 g

Total Protein: 10 g

Ingredients:

- 1 tbsp olive oil
- half tbsp crushed garlic
- 1 tbsp whole milk
- 2.3 ounces bulk turkey sausage
- ⅓ pd lean, ground beef
- 1 small egg, lightly beaten
- half tbsp minced fresh rosemary
- 2 tbsps minced fresh parsley
- half tbsp minced fresh thyme
- quarter tsp kosher salt or to taste
- 1 small shallot, minced

- 2 tbsps bread crumbs (panko)
- half tbsp Dijon mustard

Directions:

1. Turn a pan to a moderately low heat. oil is added. Add the shallot to the hot oil and cook until transparent.

2. Add the garlic and stir, cooking it until fragrant. Turn off the heat.

3. Stir together the milk and bread crumbs in a bowl. Leave alone for five minutes.

4. Combine the bread crumbs with the shallot combination, meat, sausage, rosemary, parsley, thyme, salt, and egg.

5. Divide the mixture into 12 equal sections and roll each portion into a ball.

6. Arrange the meatballs in a single layer in the air fryer basket.

7. Bake for 10 to 12 minutes, or until light brown and well cooked, in an air fryer that has been preheated to 400 °F. About halfway through baking, turn the meatballs.

8. You can either serve it as is as a snack or as the main meal with spaghetti, rice, or spiralized vegetable noodles and some sauce.

Herbed Turkey Breast

Time needed for prep: 5 minutes

Time needed to cook: 40 minutes

Serves: 4

Nutritional values per serving:

Calories: 150

Fat: 7 g

Carb: 0 g

Fiber Content: 0 g

Total Protein: 21 g

Ingredients:

- half tbsp butter, softened
- half tsp salt
- quarter tsp minced fresh sage leaves

- o   1 bone-in skin-on turkey breast piece of about 1–1half pds
- o   half tsp minced fresh thyme leaves
- o   Pepper as per taste

Directions:

1. Use parchment paper to line the air fryer basket. Spray cooking spray liberally within the air fryer basket.

2. Butter the turkey thoroughly. Add thyme, sage, salt, and pepper.

3. Arrange the turkey in the basket of the air fryer with the skin side facing up.

4. Bake for about 30 to 40 minutes, or until well cooked, in an air fryer that has been preheated to 325 °F. About halfway through baking, turn the bird. When the turkey is fully cooked, the internal temperature should be 165 °F.

5. Set your cutting board down next to the turkey. Give it a few minutes' separation.

6. Cut and present.

Turkey and Mushroom Patties

Time needed for prep: 10 minutes

Time needed to cook: 10 minutes

Serves: 10

Nutritional values per serving:

Calories: 132

Fat: 6.1 g

Carb: 3.1 g

Fiber Content: 0.5 g

Total Protein: 20.3 g

Ingredients:

- o   12 medium fresh mushrooms, quartered
- o   2 tsps garlic powder
- o   Salt as per taste
- o   2 pds extra-lean ground turkey

- o 2 tbsps Maggi seasoning sauce
- o Pepper as per taste
- o Cooking spray

Directions:

1. Fill the food processor bowl with the mushrooms. Until it is chopped, process.

2. Blend all the ingredients except the turkey and pulse several times to thoroughly combine.

3. Place inside a dish. Make a thorough, hand-mixed addition of the turkey. The mixture shouldn't be kneaded because doing so will make the meat tough.

4. Divide the mixture into 10 equal amounts, then form each portion into patties. Each patty should have a divot in the middle.

5. Cooking spray should be applied on both sides of the patties. Put the patties in a single layer in the air fryer basket. Make batches of food.

6. Air fry at 320 °F for 10 minutes, or until the desired doneness, in an air fryer that has been preheated. Halfway through frying, flip the sides.

7. Distribute hot over lettuce leaves, on buns, or simply as is.

Olive-Brined Air-Fryer Turkey Breast

Time needed for prep: 5 minutes

Time needed to cook: 20 minutes

Serves: 7

Nutritional values per serving:

Calories: 141

Fat: 0.9 g

Carb: 1.4 g

Fiber Content: 0.6 g

Total Protein: 30.2 g

Ingredients:

- o 6 tbsps brine from canned olives
- o 1.75 pds boneless, skinless turkey breast
- o 1 sprig fresh thyme

- o   quarter cup buttermilk
- o   Fresh rosemary

Directions:

1. In a basin, mix together the buttermilk and brine.

2. Put a zip-top bag with the turkey breast inside. Seal the bag after adding the buttermilk mixture, rosemary, and thyme. After giving the bag a few turns, chill for 7-8 hours.

3. 30 minutes before cooking, remove the bag from the fridge.

4. Fry for about 10-15 minutes, or until the desired doneness, in an air fryer that has been preheated to 350 °F. Halfway through frying, flip the sides.

5. The meat's internal temperature should be 165 °F.

Greek Turkey Burgers

Time needed for prep: 10 minutes

Time needed to cook: 15 minutes

Serves: 4

Nutritional values per serving:

Calories: 351

Fat: 16 g

Carb: 26 g

Fiber Content: 4 g

Total Protein: 28 g

Ingredients:

- o   16 ounces turkey breast
- o   4 tsps chopped fresh oregano
- o   half tsp salt
- o   1 cup spinach leaves (small)
- o   1 tbsp red wine vinegar

- o 4 whole-wheat burger buns, split, toasted
- o 3 tbsps extra-virgin olive oil
- o 1 tsp crushed red pepper
- o 4 cloves garlic, peeled, grated
- o half cup thinly sliced red onion
- o half cup crumbled feta cheese
- o Cooking spray
- o Any other toppings of your choice

Directions:

1. Spray cooking spray in the basket of the air fryer.

2. Combine the turkey with the oregano, garlic, oil, salt, and pepper in a basin.

3. Divide the mixture into 4 equal amounts and form patties from them (about half inch in thickness).

4. Insert the air fryer basket with the patties inside. If necessary, cook in batches.

5. Fry for 13–15 minutes, or until the desired doneness, in an air fryer that has been preheated to 360 °F. Halfway through frying, flip the sides.

6. The meat's internal temperature should be 155 °F.

7. In a bowl, combine the vinegar and onion.

8. Top the bottom half of the patties with feta cheese. Put spinach on top of it.

9. Top it with a hamburger. Slices of onion go here. if using, place tomato slices here. If using, drizzle mayonnaise.

10. Top with the burger's top half.

Turkey-Stuffed Peppers

Time needed for prep: 15 minutes

Time needed to cook: 10 minutes per batch

Serves: 6

Nutritional values per serving:

Calories: 407

Fat: 21 g

Carb: 26 g

Fiber Content: 4 g

Total Protein: 29 g

Ingredients:

- o 6 medium red or yellow bell peppers, halved lengthwise, deseeded
- o 24 ounces ground turkey
- o half cup bread crumbs (panko)
- o 6 tbsps chopped parsley
- o half cup parmesan cheese (grated)
- o 2 tbsps olive oil
- o 1 cup cooked brown rice
- o 1half cups low-sodium marinara sauce
- o Pepper as per taste
- o half cup shredded mozzarella

Directions:

1. Spray cooking spray in the basket of the air fryer.

2. Heat up a skillet to a medium-high temperature. oil is added. Once the oil is hot, add the turkey and brown it. As it cooks, break it simultaneously.

3. Thoroughly combine the bread crumbs and rice. For one minute, cook. Turn off the heat.

4. Stir in the pepper, parsley, and Parmesan cheese with the marinara sauce.

5. Distribute the mixture equally among the bell pepper halves. Make batches of food.

6. Arrange the pepper halves in the basket of the air fryer.

7. Bake peppers for 8 to 9 minutes, or until they are soft, in an air fryer that has been preheated to 350 °F.

8. Top with mozzarella cheese. To get the cheese to melt, cook for a few more minutes.

Almond-Crusted Turkey Cutlets

Time needed for prep: 10 minutes

Time needed to cook: 20 minutes

Serves: 2

Nutritional values per serving:

Calories: 279

Fat: 11.3 g

Carb: 5.5 g

Fiber Content: 3.4 g

Total Protein: 40.5 g

Ingredients:

- o 2 turkey cutlets (5 ounces each)
- o White of a small egg
- o 1 tbsp lukewarm water
- o quarter tsp garlic powder
- o Pepper as per taste
- o Salt as per taste
- o ⅓ cup almond flour
- o 1 tsp rosemary
- o quarter tsp oregano herbs (dry)
- o 1 tsp extra-virgin olive oil

Directions:

1. Spray cooking spray in the basket of the air fryer.

2. In a bowl, mix together the egg white and water.

3. In a small bowl, combine the almond flour, salt, pepper, dried herbs, and seasoning. Stir.

4. Dip the cutlet into the egg mixture first. Shake to remove any extra egg. Dredge in the flour mixture after that. To adhere, lightly press. Shake the extra flour mixture off.

5. Set the air fryer to cook the cutlets.

6. Fry for 13–15 minutes, or until the desired doneness, in an air fryer that has been preheated to 330 °F. Halfway through frying, flip the sides.

7. The meat's internal temperature should be 155 °F.

8. If wanted, serve with baked potatoes and a green salad.

Conclusion

Thank you for reading Air Fryer For Beginners all the way to the end; I hope it was helpful and gave you the tools you needed to accomplish any objectives you may have had.

The air fryer is a favorite among many people due to its various conveniences. It makes cleaning really simple. The air fryer is adaptable while also being quiet, quick, and saving a ton of time during cooking. For instance, cooking frozen items in an oven can take longer than 20 minutes, whereas cooking them in an air fryer will only take a half-hour or less.

Additionally, unlike frying in a skillet or baking in an oven, using this equipment won't cause your kitchen to become overheated. The main benefit, though, is that you can fry using a far healthier technique and up to 75% less fat! So it's beneficial to use an air fryer for regular cooking. It looks out for your health without sacrificing flavor.

So now is the time to replace your conventional pan or oven with an air fryer and rediscover your love for fried meals while still being mindful of your health.

Again, thank you for selecting this book, and best of luck to you in all of your future cooking ventures.

Made in United States
Troutdale, OR
04/24/2024

19362693R30093